CONTENTS

ACKNOWLEDGEMENTS

Deep gratitude to the supportive group of female friends listed in my on-line address book as 'gal pals'. They were the early recipients of some of these writings and their enthusiastic and encouraging responses pushed me to do more than I ever thought I could: Diane Amidon, Ruth Anderson, Judy Arthofer, Pat Bailey, Jarel Bartig, Diane Birnbaum, Jane Bodenhamer, Kay Braun, Fran Christensen, Jane Dinkmeyer, Patti Gilbert, Cheryl Gingerich, Suzanne Goddard, Marie Harrington, Lyn Hall, Cindy Hartley, Diane Hundley, Dee Irwin, Karen Kelly, Nancy Kraft, Carole LeBar, Mary Lee, Jeri Madsen, Sally Marion, Mae Miner, Bonnie Roth, and Brenda Tuckey. I must also add several special male friends to this list: Todd Drake, Jerry Straszheim, Phil Stringer, and Alan Wenrich.

Heartfelt gratitude to the many parts and persons of my family, especially to my children- Hope Sutton, Mark Sutton, and Paul Griffin- all of whom have patiently nurtured me and continue to grant me the grace of forgiving my faults and foibles and celebrating my creative craziness.

But most of all, thanks to fellow pilgrim and anam cara, Sally Marion, who responded to my earlier book, *New Day Dawning,* with, "Now I want a poem for every day of the year," which prompted and prodded this writing more than she will ever know.

I love and appreciate you, one and all.

FORWARD...

I know- the correct word here is 'foreword': the author's explanatory notes, comments, to you, the reader, concerning the book you are about to read. But this writing work has been a journey for me, as I hope the reading will be for you.

I did not intend, as I embarked on this trek, this daily pilgrimage, to write an autobiography, a memoir, and yet, what has resulted from nearly two years of effort is a kind of road map through my life, as I have found myself revealing in my writing the person I have become and the road taken to get there.

And always, ever, the journey leads forward- around the next turn, into the next day. Though the destination is uncertain, I continue on the journey- and I invite you to come along for company.

JANUARY -
the year begins

January 1 - New Year's Day

The beginning of a new year is a time of reflection- looking back...looking forward- but most of all, being grateful for where you are right now. All that has gone before has brought you to this moment, this place, this point of view...ever becoming...ever changing...ever new and renewed. Rejoice! The year begins.

the gift

I have a gift...
the wrapping isn't much
but the contents-
   oh, the contents!
It takes my breath away
   to see the gift inside.
My cautious adult heart
doubts it is really mine
and turns away,
      unsure of what to do,
      now that the lid is off.
      "No returns now,"
      it thinks...
         despairing, fearful...
But then the Child-
the joyful
   irrepressible
   lovely Child
     grabs hold the gift
     and laughing
       dancing
       singing
     celebrates what has
     been given.
   "Let's play! she cries.
   "Let's play!"

You have to be willing to step into a mysterious unknown situation and listen to the creative response within you, whether it be music, the voice of wisdom, or a calling to just be spontaneous.
-Rachel Bagby

January 2

We are shaped by words...words do matter. What they mean...how we use them...how we give them life with voice, pen, computer keyboard. And sometimes, what is really meant by what we say is unclear...as our words seem to take on a life of their own. Speak carefully, thoughtfully, lovingly, as you birth your words to life.

abandon

'Abandon' has a
thoroughly nasty
connotation...
   leaving something or someone
   precious & worthy behind
   without a backward glance...
   running away from...
   devaluing by departing...

But living with abandon-
ah! that is something
else entirely...
   yielding to the impulsive
   child within...
   acting with spontaneity...
   choosing the path of
   lightheartedness in
   spite of circumstances
   which belittle its truth...

Odd, isn't it, how
one word can go
in totally opposite
directions...
pulling mind & heart...
shaping life & choice...
demanding thoughtfulness
                and honesty.

We are here to live out loud. **-Honore Balzac**

January 3

A birthday is a special gift- whenever it comes in the year, whatever the age being celebrated. A day to recall, with awe and amazement, the wonder of your being, the beauty of your presence in this world. For in all of the ages of time, in the countless numbers of human lives which have gone before you, YOU are a unique being, your life a gift to be cherished and lived fully.

birthday prayer
This is MY day...
a day to celebrate...
a day to rejoice...
a day to cherish the wonder.
I don't know where I'm going-
  at least, not exactly-
and I surely need guidance
  along the way.
Hold my hand, Brother Christ.
Walk with me.
Speak your call directly
  into my ear as, step by step,
  I follow the path
      in front of me.
Re-birth me, Spirit of Life.
        LET IT BE SO- today & every day.

Just to be is a blessing.
Just to live is holy.
        -Abraham Heschel

January 4
Be bold. If you're going to make an error, make it a doozy. **-Billie Jean King**

AUDACITY
AUDACIOUS!
outrageous!
daring!
caring!
standing my ground,
  not out of stubbornness,
  but out of commitment.
AUDACIOUS!
courageous!
daring!
sharing!
speaking my mind- and heart...

willing to be misunderstood.
AUDACIOUS!
contagious!
daring!
wearing my heart on
    my sleeve...and
    reaching out to invite
    others to share the
    journey-
        if they dare.

January 5

W O M A N

Who said I am less
    because my gender is
    female? less intelligent
                less talented
                less able to lead
                less able to make decisions?
Outrageous!
    I represent more than
    half the human race.
Made in the image of
    the Divine...
        given the power to
            bear life...
            create beauty...
            speak loving truth...
And revel in the
    loveliness and strength
    that is my body...
            my mind...
            my spirit...
                without apology!
Now is the time for
    women everywhere-
    and men, too-
        to affirm equality...
            to celebrate differences...

to respect the unique
contribution we
each and all make
to the fullness of life.
NOW IS THE TIME!

January 6

My life continues to be impacted & shaped by the seasons of the church year, as well as by Nature's seasons. There is a certain holiness in honoring the ways in which the pace of life changes with the seasons- when we open our awareness to their presence in our lives.

worship

Worship...hearts &
minds & voices united
in prayer & praise...
a mighty "YES"
offered to the One
Who Loves, the One
Who Creates by
gathered co-creators...
the Word heard,
ingested, & enfleshed
as ordinary people
are transformed by
the unifying power of
scripture read...bread &
wine shared...the kiss
of peace...
    blessed
    empowered
    sent into their worlds
    to BE the Light
    they came to see &
        feel &
        experience...
           Epiphany!

January 7

Camouflage is a game we all like to play, but our secrets are as surely revealed by what we want to seem to be as by what we want to conceal. -Russell Lynes

masks...

The masks I wear,
the roles I play-
all stand in the way
of revelation-
of opening up my
really, truly self
to be known & seen...
accepted & rejected...
loved & hated...
admired & despised...
Sometimes I keep the mask in place
because I do not dare to risk...
my inner self
too fragile for the
"slings & arrows of
outrageous fortune"-
the world's response
to soul-baring
vulnerability...
Sometimes I strut upon the stage,
clad in the role which suits me best
at that moment in time...
acting as if...
posturing...
being who I think
the many "yous" inhabiting
my world expect me to be...
But sometimes...sometimes
I let myself be seen...
reveal the inner truth
of who & how I am...
share my gifts
speak my truth
take the risk-
and, oh, the joy!

7.

January 8

morning grace

Thank you, Adonai,
for your presence
in and around me...
for the love you
inspire and the
inspiration you
      love into being.
Grant me a clean heart
and a clear vision
      this day...
  a sense of hopefulness
     and love...
  an awareness of the
      holiness of every moment &
      all of life.
Let peace penetrate
my world...
let hope fill my heart...
let understanding enliven
  my choices & undergird
     my words.
        IT IS ENOUGH.

January 9

wandering

I wander as I wonder...
  roaming far afield,
  leaving the well-trod path...
    as I follow my bliss
    as I follow the questions
    and doubts pulling
     me this way & that...

I wander as I wonder...
  choosing the road less
    traveled...

clawing my way
through thorns and
brambles which
block the path to
  Truth...

I wander as I wonder...
  mind & heart filled with
  the questions which will
  not go away...
    who am I really?
    how did I come to be?
    where am I headed?
    which path shall I take?
        and
    who is God, anyway?

And all I know for sure is
  the wondering will never
    cease...
  the wandering will never
    end...
      So be it. Amen

January 10

If the only prayer you say in your whole life is 'thank you',
that would suffice. **-Meister Eckhart**

today's blessings

For the blessing of this day of life,
  I give thanks.
For a comfortable bed & the roof
  over my head,
    I give thanks.
For sight & hearing, speech & thought,
  touch & awareness, pain & pleasure,
    I give thanks.
For friends & family, elders &
  children, neighbors & strangers,
    I give thanks.

For a gradually-aging body,
   for wrinkles & cellulite,
   for aches & pains reminding
   me I am ALIVE,
     I give thanks.
For books & music, for art &
   artists, for the power & gift
   of beauty,
     I give thanks.
For hope when all seems hopeless,
   for light within the darkness,
   for joy that shines through tears.
   for hands & hearts that
   reach out to hold & comfort,
     I give thanks.

On *this* day,
   at *this* moment,
     I am thankful...
        and it is enough.

January 11

God is everything which is good, as I see it, and the goodness which everything has is God. -Julian of Norwich

the with-ness of God

I dwell in the with-ness
   of God...
      God in me...
      me in God...
transparent
wide open
   a window, clean
   of finger marks and
   smudges...
      welcoming the light...
      providing clear &
      unobstructed views
      of the divine...
   a window, thrust
   open wide so

all the winds of life & spirit
can blow through...
and in...
stirring up the
settled dust that
dims the beauty
of life's color & joy.

May my words
be that window for you...
as I step aside to let you
see the beauty & reality of
God in you...
and God in me...
and God in all...
a trinity of sorts...
truly holy
truly whole
wholly divine.

January 12

One of the most wonderful, fullest parts of life, of friendship, is to be able to hold dear friends in heart and mind, to be entrusted to share not only their joys but their pains & sorrows- and to know that they will also do the same for you. How amazing! How beautiful!

for Sally

At the other end of morning, evening...
at the other end of dusk is dawn...
at the other end of living, dying...
at the other end of come is gone.

The reality of life is new beginnings...
the reality of life is death...
And in between, the stuff of living-
the hope & pain of every passing breath.

At the other end of morning, evening...
at the other end of darkness, light...
at the other end of solitude, a friend's hand
that reaches through the soul's dark, lonely night.

The reality of life is journeys taken...
the reality of life- the daring choice
to blaze a trail that others have forsaken,
to rise and still rejoice-
  YES, I AM ALIVE & THIS IS LIVING!
    THIS IS MY LIFE!

January 13

I find myself writing a great deal about writing...one of the most significant parts of my self, of my life. Again and again, I wrestle with the desire to put my words on paper- and the fear inherent in doing just that.

open...

Open the eyes of my heart,
  O God...
Open my intellect,
  Spirit of Truth...
Draw me on the path of
  real life...
    reveal your Presence
    to me in the every-day.
Help me to affirm the one-ness
  of all creation...
  the with-ness of your
  creative energy...
to see myself as a conduit
  for that creativity...
    a place of transparency
    and openness...
  that in & through me,
    your truth may be seen...experienced...
                apprehended...enjoyed.
  For in my writing,
  I am a servant...
    open to the breath of
    the divine that flows
      through & in & around me...
        and so I write.

Breaking silence changes the world. -**Christina Baldwin**

January 14

Awaken your spirit to adventure;
Hold nothing back, learn to find ease in risk;
Soon you will be home in a new rhythm.
For your soul senses the world that awaits you.
                                                    -John O'Donohue

in balance

My younger sister used to
walk a balance beam...
twist & turn & leap
on that five-inch path
leading to- nowhere...
        back & forth she went,
        life reduced- for that
        brief time- to focus on
        not falling off...
        on executing complicated
        feats of acrobatic skill
        while balanced on
        a beam of wood...
        maintaining her lovely
                equilibrium & poise.
And sometimes, in the
passing years, I have
found myself on a narow path,
seeking, yearning for
        that same sense of focus,
        that same skill of balance
                as I try to execute
                complicated feats
                of daily living,
        trying not to fail & fall...
        trying to maintain my
                equilibrium & pull off life
                with some small measure
                        of poise...
                                mind,
                                body,
                                spirit
                                BALANCED.   13.

January 15

All mystery is about the dark.
All darkness is about mystery. -Matthew Fox

darkness

Darkness, thick & total...
no sign of the morning sun,
no sound of morning bird...
only dark silence-
    and I am immersed in it...
        lost in it...
    Discouragement & despair
    come easily in the darkness...
    the sense that light will
    never, ever break through...
    the sense that hope has fled,
    never, ever to return...

Yet I know this is not true.
At the distant horizon, a
hint of daylight to come...
   the barest glint, it's true,
   but a promise of the
     day beginning anew.

And here in my room, a tiny
candle adds its steady light,
the flame tall & unwavering,
a reminder of
the Presence which persists in
spite of my doubts...
the Ever-Presence which
surrounds & fills & blesses me
with the incredible, hopeful gift
of a new day.

    What other response can I
    give but "thank you"...
    with the whispered pledge to
    use it wisely & well.
        Let it be so.

14.

January 16

wilderness

Lead me as I
stumble in the wilderness,
          O God.
Help me to understand
that I can find comfort
   in the darkness...
   and safety, as well as
   fear & threat.
Sometimes I need the
protective presence of night
   to cover me...
sometimes the light is
simply too bright for my
   tear-filled eyes.
Perhaps darkness is not
so much about the
inability to see or understand,
   but rather about the need
   for comfort & nurture...
      a return to the womb,
      the source of life.
And perhaps we lose our
night vision as we age
   because there is
      too much light.
        I wonder...

January 17

Struggle is a vital part of the spiritual journey, as uncomfortable as it often feels. Questions and doubts mark the path and it is only in looking back that we find there the times & places of greatest growth.

distance

Today You seem
so far away...
    and I do not
    know who You are.
How much simpler,
really, to adopt the
generally-accepted
    biblical image whole-cloth...
      to *not* question...
      to slip into the mode
      of religious life which
      says everything is
      wonderful as long as
        "Jesus is Lord."
Only **that is not true.**
My daughter feels lost & alone...
my son feels hopeless...
my niece is in pain & suffers
greatly...
    and I can do nothing
      but PRAY?!
How schizophrenic this whole
  God-thing is...
      I believe;
      Help my unbelief.
        HELP!!!

*Remember that the faith that moves mountains
always carries a pick.* **-Anonymous**

January 18

*Writing is reverse incarnation-
Flesh Made Word.*
-Margaret Atwood

re-vision
A change of venue...
sitting in my
basement den...my lair...
surrounded by music and
candlelight...darkness fills
the window before me as
the day has not yet fully
begun...
birds are silent, and only the
ticking of the clock marks
the passing moments.
I come seeking a new
perspective...a different view
of the world...to open
myself to new possibilities...
to invite the Creative
Spirit to reveal herself
in a new way...to see again
the world in which I live &
move & have my being as if
for the first time...
                    to write!

January 19

presents
Your presence is my
   present today...
        the gift of peace...
        the gift of awareness...
        the gift of quiet joy...

Your presence is my
   present today...
        the gift of blessing...

the gift of hope...
the gift of anticipation...
Your presence is my
present today...
the gift of wonder...
the gift of creativity...
the gift of love...
May each moment
be filled with
unwrapping the
present...
each breath an
awareness of
the NOW...
and when the day comes
to a close,
GRATITUDE!

January 20

Because everything we do and everything we are is in jeopardy, and because the peril is immediate and unremitting, every person is the right person to act and every moment is the right moment to begin.
-Jonathan Schell

planetary shift

The axis of the world
has shifted...
from trust to fear...
from co-creation to destruction...
from on-going life to annihilation...

And now it *must* shift again...
from division to one-ness...
from enmity to relationship...
from cynicism to wonder...
from death to new life...

The clarion call for change echoes
from the mountains, scarred by
wildfires & indiscriminate mining...
from the rivers, polluted

by industrial & animal waste...
from the inner cities, neglected
    and forgotten except by those
    who thrive on darkness
    of streets & lives...
from the silenced voices of
    children, abused & used
    to increase the profit
    margin of business,
    for the gratification of
        unspeakable desires...

            It must ring & echo in the halls
            of Congress...of every State House...
            in the White House, getting
            louder & louder & louder,
                until the axis of the world
                shifts again.

January 21

Today is what we have...today & only today. And yet, we live as if this life would go on forever. THIS is the day we have...to use, to waste, to cherish... the choice is ours...the choice is MINE.

down...

Thursday was a "down" day for me...though
I really don't know why...perhaps because
the flow of words has stopped- dammed up
                            run dry
diverted into something else of which I am unable,
    unwilling to speak.
Why this reluctance to give voice to what I feel?
Perhaps because I don't even know what
that is, at this particular moment of my life,
as with my astigmatic eyes, I gaze
into a future blurred,
    distorted by my point of view.
Clarity, O God...clarity & wisdom...
and the hope & trust to let the future hold itself,
        while I speak in the present tense.

January 22

*We do not choose a vision, we are not given a longing, unless
we are also given the ability to fulfill it.* -Christina Baldwin

freedom

Am I willing to take the risks of freedom-
to define "discipleship" and "leadership"
for myself, rather than conforming
to the ideas and opinions of others?
Do I fear seeing what others
do *not* see? Yes & no...
   yes, because I fear being misunderstood,
      being seen as "peculiar" or "crazy"...
   no, because what I see is *real* ...what
     I know is *truth*...what I experience
     is an unfolding, ongoing journey-
       and I would not go back to where I was!

Of course the steps are often
fearsome...looking back over
my shoulder can bring longing
for other times & places...
   but always the Holy Presence
          pulls...
          tugs...
          pushes...
          prods...
          leads.

Being in step with
the Divine can mean-
often *does* mean- being
   out-of-step with everyone else...
     not in arrogance but
     in all humility...
       allowing others to be
       where *they* are as I am
         where *I* am...

January 23

'There is no such thing as a stupid question." How many times did I hear that from teachers over the years? But somehow, when we become adults, it seems we are supposed to have the answers- and I find that what I have are more & more & more questions!

question

Quench not

Uncertainty.

Questioning is at the heart of spiritual journeying.
-Gregg Levoy

Entertain possibility and

Speak out your truth,

Testament to the gift of Divine Creativity

Inside, around, flowing through you & your life.

Open your mind, heart, eyes, ears to the world around you &

Never, ever stop questioning!

January 24

There is no one right way. No one has the only way to God, to love, or to spiritual truth.
-Michael Lerner

not enough

Why the competition
for God? For isn't that what
the Holy Wars between
Christian sects, between
Moslem and Christian
and Jew are really all
about? Each group
demanding God for itself,
as if the Divine
is not big enough to
encompass *every* heart, *every*
life...

 each group defining God
 for itself, in *its own image*,
 as if the Divine can be
 captured & encapsulated by

human limitations...
each group fearfully
guarding its "truth", as if the
Divine Truth can be pared
down to human size.
And is this because we are really
so fearful that there is not
enough of God to
go around?
I wonder...

January 25

Sometimes in very old bodies there are incredibly young, wild souls looking out at you. -John O'Donohue

mom

I look deeply at my mother
and try to see parts of myself...
And there they are-
       the reader
       the loner
       the lover of words
       the loyal friend
But at ninety-plus, her
'do-er' self has almost
disappeared. I remember
her well...driven always-
   or so it seemed-
   by doing what was right...
   putting her own desires on hold...
   shaped by others, by
   the circumstances of her life...
   ever & always, the
     'good girl'...
the ultra-responsible
   oldest child.
And as I gaze into the soul's
   mirror, I wonder just whose life
     I am describing...

22.

January 26

The universe is change; our life is what our thoughts make it.
-Marcus Aurelius

life happens
Life happens
moment by moment,
not once and done but
little by little

January 27

now...
Who knows how many
   years lie ahead of me?
      what they will bring?
What I have is *now-*
      who I am
      what I have learned
            through living my life.
And a gift for words...
      my own "voice"...

Creative Spirit, inspire
me to begin anew with
this new year...
   to re-order and re-new
   and re-energize...
   to open myself to the
   holiness & wholeness of my life,
      however it plays
      itself out.

I wrap my arms around,
embrace, accept
      the gift of this day.

*I choose to inhabit my days, to
allow my living to open me.*
-Dawna Markova

23.

January 28

Let us look for secret things somewhere in the world on the blue shore of silence. -**Pablo Neruda**

wonder...

I did not see your face
  in the wind-
    I admit it-
but I was awed
    by the power
    by the strength-
and isn't that a bit
    of the same thing?
        I wonder...

January 29

May we be helped to do whatever is most right.
-**Traditional American Indian prayer**

integrity

O God of Integrity,
    how often I mouth the words
    which sound correct...
    express indignation at the
    policies of my government,
    the decisions of my church- but DO nothing.
Frozen...
    immobilized by the
    overwhelming reality of
    need in this world, I DO nothing.
Oh, I pray...
    you know I pray, O God,
    flinging my words & thoughts
    into the universe we all inhabit...
    yet how often those
        prayers are simply
        wails of grief &
        impatience &
        childish angst...
    while pen & paper lie unused...

phone calls to those in Congress
go unmade...
choices about how to spend-
                    money
                    time
                    attention
                    compassion-
lack deliberation,
avoid responsibility...

Yet here I am,
a living incarnation
of a holy spirit...
        holding in my
        hands & life the
          power to choose...
                    to co-create...
                    to be a part of
                            making justice...
                    of saying yes
                            to life...

Help me to say- and mean-
  "Here I am- use me!"
                    AMEN

January 30
*Sometimes the questions which arise as I read & think & write are not easily answered. In fact, I **ask** much more easily than I answer. Perhaps you do, too.*

imago dei
How much of "God"
have I made in the
image I *need* God to be?
And is this idolatry-
        or simply
            being human?

January 31

Sometimes, when we least expect it, when life seems at it lowest ebb, we are gifted with a surprise which fills us with hope & delight...the wonder of grace.

blooming winter

Hidden in a corner of my yard,
    daffodils are blooming,
lured by the deceptive
warmth of winter
    gone awry.
They sprang to life almost
overnight,
    waving sun-drenched
    heads in breezes
    soon turned cold.
Yet still they bloom,
in spite of freezing nights
    and wind-tossed days.
From their protected niche
they radiate a shining
    ray of color in the
    midst of garden's
    winter gloom,
waving a courageous flag
    of joy and hope,
    of promised spring
    in spite of winter's cold.

We tire of just seeing. What we want is vision to be able to name that which we see as a manifestation of grace. **-Marv Hiles**

reflections...

26.

FEBRUARY -
winter continues

February 1

Writing makes a person very vulnerable. It opens you to public criticism, to ridicule, to rejection. But it also opens conversation and thought. It stirs minds, and touches hearts. It brings us into contact with our souls. So how can it possibly be a waste of time, an idle act, a mistake, a betrayal of truth? Who can possibly tell us not to do it? -Joan Chittister

writing...

Every time I write,
   I lay my self on the line...
   present my self
   as a sacrifice
   on the altar of
      judgment...
      criticism...
      evaluation by others.
Every time I write,
   I open my heart, bare my soul,
   take the risk of
      revelation...
      vulnerability...
      transparency.
Every time I write,
   I join my self with
   the Creative Divine...claiming
   my place as co-creator...
   celebrating my role
   in healing creation...
      emboldened...
      audacious...
      awestruck.
Every time I write,
   I have a vision
   of journeys shared...
   of hearts & hands & lives joined
      in love & celebration...
      in pain & grief & sadness...
  of Oneness
    Wholeness
    Holiness...
      and so I write on...

February 2

All being itself is derived from God and the presence of the Creator is in each created thing. -**Rabbi Menachem Nahum**

where is God?

God is fully present-
or present fully-
   in ALL of life...
and the unveiling
   of the faces of God
   never ends...
Revelation keeps
   happening...
      on-going...
      continual...
         reminding me
            there is no WHERE
            God is not...

Fully-present God,
   keep me mindful
   as I live
   this day-
         the hours &
            the moments...
         the space of
            every breath...

Keep me alert
         curious
         aware...
Let me live with
   eyes & heart
     open wide.

This IS a day of my
   life- a place &
   space where we
   meet & relate- you & I...
Let me live it well.
         Amen & amen

February 3

Though some would call it a cliché, I believe life is a journey. From that first dramatic adventure of birth to the great unknown of death, we live & move with a sense of 'something more'... 'somewhere else'... always seeking that place, that state, we call 'home'.

journey

To be human is
to be a sojourner...
    a nomad...
    a pilgrim...
        unsure of where and how
        we began...but drawn,
        guided, pushed, propelled by
        a sense of 'going home'...
        a yearning for that place & presence
           from which we first emerged, our inner
           magnet homing in on that guiding star,
           the Due North which leads to Holy Truth...
               step by step by step...
               day by day by day...

The person is always a nomad, journeying from threshold to threshold, into ever different experiences. **–John O'Donohue**

February 4

beginning again...

My day begins...
alone & yet joined...
apart & together...
always & ever the paradox of
        beginning & ending...
Let today be a celebration
of ordinary things...
of commonplace
  tasks...
of the blessing of
  sharing. IT IS ENOUGH!

30.

February 5

In saying yes to our calls, we bring flesh to word and form to faith. -**Gregg Levoy**

imago dei II

Imagination

Manifesting

Audaciously

Gloriously

Outrageously
Our

Destiny

Emerging

In creativity

THIS is what it means
to be created in the image
of God...to give life & expression
to the Divine Within Us...
Are you listening?
The voice of Divine Creativity
is calling your name!

February 6

The world is at war...and fear pervades the landscape of our days. And in the midst of it all, I think and wonder...and ask questions- of myself, of my country, of my fellow planetary pilgrims.

WAR

Is the world at war because
within ourselves,
we are at war?
Unable, unwilling
to make peace with
unanswered questions...
unable, unwilling
to live without having
all the answers...
reaching out to grasp &

clasp because we fear
there is not enough...
            not enough food...
            not enough power...
            not enough energy...
            not enough love...
Because we have not learned
to share, we see others as
the "enemy"...fighting tooth & nail
    for our own portion of the
    universe's abundant
    providence...
instead of reaching out
    to lend a hand...
    to share a meal...
    to sing a song of hope
        amidst the rubble
        left by war and fighting
        and hopelessness...
When will we learn
there IS enough?
When will we learn
to share?

February 7

Writing is like living. It requires boldness and a deep dedication to my own truth. It means being willing to plumb the depths of my soul and then take the risk of spreading out my treasures- some quite beautiful, others odd and misshapen- for others to see. It means speaking in my own voice, one that is uniquely mine, that belongs to me alone. It is hard work- and ultimate joy.

my own voice

Writing is about
finding my own "voice"...
    so easy for the birds,
    it seems...they open their
    mouths and out tumble
    their own songs...
        authentically theirs...
    a wren's song always
        a wren's...

a towhee singing only
            a towhee song...
                    and it does not matter
                    who's listening...
Would that it were so easy for me!
Can I give voice to
my own story? write about
                        grief survived
                        my spiritual journey
                        family relationships
                        healing a broken heart
        from my own point of view,
        without worrying about
        how it will be heard by others?
Can I be true to myself
                on paper?

February 8

Companions who can share our experience and insights are
essential on the inward quest. -Jacquelyn Small

today

Breathing in life deeply...
the pungent aroma of fresh
    coffee...
the flickering light of a
    votive candle...
the early-morning chill creeping
    beneath the blanket covering
    my legs...
Today & today & today...
    each one new & fresh-
        a clean slate
        a sparkling sheet of white paper
            on which to write
            the moments of my life...
Live and reflect...reflect and live...
    I know no other way...
        with an occasional friend
        for company on the road...
            and IT IS ENOUGH.

February 9

God is a creator. God's being, God's life is the source of all that is. God is constantly bringing into being that which was not, that which is new.
—Gordon Cosby

God's will

"What is God's will for my life?"
How often, as a pastor, I have heard
   this question- or
     asked it myself-
  as if there were an
     answer...THE answer...
  as if a finger writing
     on the wall or
  a voice from the
    clouds or
  a bush aflame
     in our path
  will tell us
     that truth!

Perhaps what God-
   the Divine, the Ground
  of Being- wills for us
  is to be truly
       fully
       totally who we are!
    our beauty & frailty...
    our light & darkness...
    our kindness & cruelty...
    our hope & despair...
       without knowing
       where or why or how,
       but only knowing
         that we *are*...
         and the Divine
         comes into being
         again & again
         through us...
         and to know that
           IT IS ENOUGH!

February 10

I love to be surrounded by, bathed in, music. Since my early childhood when the sounds of the piano, being played by my mother, my aunt, my uncle, were part of daily life, music has enlivened, inspired, supported, comforted me. And whether I am singing or whistling or dancing along, I am borne up by this incredible gift of another's talent, an awesome gift of Divine Creativity...and I celebrate!

music

I need to play
music...
   to let it flow
      through me...
     enliven me...
For life IS music.
All things have
   their own rhythm...
   their own beat
      of life...
Story & sound...
words & music...
heart & soul...
   bearing me up,
     higher & higher...
   resonating deep,
     deep within...
      an echo of
      the voice of God.
The melody flows...
the rhythm
   resounds...
   drawing me
   irresistibly into
     the dance
      of life...
     singing at the
TOP OF MY VOICE!!!

February 11

How do I want to be remembered? What is most significant about my life? These questions greeted me this morning and would not let me go without an answer...

remember me...

Remember me,
  my beloved ones,
as one who lived
  well & fully,
    if not always wisely...
as one who tried
  to be authentically
    myself...
as one who practiced
  acceptance (not always
  with success) and tried
  to provide an atmosphere
    for growth...
as one who took risks,
  occasionally jumping
  without a safety net,
  certain I could fly...
as one who was resilient,
  who could not be
  crushed by the hard,
  heavy places of life...
as one who lived from
  a place of deep faith-
  shaped by heritage,
  honed by experience,
  celebrated with arms
    wide open...
as one who practiced
  forgiveness, sometimes
  coming to it only
  after great internal
  struggle- but coming to it
    nevertheless...
as one who offered & accepted &
    cherished friendship

as one of the greatest gifts
  of my life…
as one whose children &
  grandchildren were
  the heart of who I was-
  always standing in awe
  of the fact that
    my blood flowed
    through their veins…
    my DNA was part
    of them…
as one who always
  asked questions…
  sought knowledge…
  was never bored…
as one who lived without
  having all the answers,
  understanding that
  Mystery is at the core
    of human existence &
    Divine Presence…
as one who loved life and
  left this existence
  only with great
  reluctance, yet
  with the certainty
  that there is still more
  to come-
        somewhere
        somehow…

…we can still leave footprints in a trail
whose end we do not know.
-Annie Dillard

February 12

Not just your best self finds God. All of you does.
-Deepak Chopra

mixed metaphors...

Journey inward,
journey outward,
          coalesce...
     they are parallel...
     they are one-
          if there is any integrity
          to them at all...
They have congruity:
     as we go deeper, we go wider-
          in our reach
               our influence...
Life is nothing
     if not a YES to
     the God-force that
     dwells within and
                    without...
     and every piece of life
          every experience
          every emotion
          every tear
          every failure
          every joy
          every pain
     is part of the
     magnificent panorama
     we are painting with
          the brush and palette
                         of living.

reflections...

38.

February 13

...the narrative of our lives is written in the small, the simple,
and the common. The overlooked. The discarded. The reclaimed.
Life is not made up of minutes, hours, days, weeks, months, or years,
but of moments. You must experience each one before you can appreciate it.
-Sarah Ban Breathnach

simplicity

We want things simple, don't we?
want things down pat...
want answers to life's questions...
want clarity instead of paralyzing fog...
want ease instead of pain...
want a road map for life's
    tortuous & twisting road...
want to have it all instead of
    being in need...
And then the laser beam of the unexpected
cuts through the detritus of life and etches
a cross on your heart...
    and the light breaks through!

February 14

valentine snowfall

A delicious, delightful
taste of winter...
nature's surprise party of
swirling snowflake confetti,
the trees draped with sparkling
white, while a pristine carpet
spreads beneath my dancing feet...
the world a lacy Valentine
singing, 'I love you' to its, sleepy,
nodding, often-oblivious
human denizens,
    while the birds flock in wide-awake,
    joyous abandon to the newly-filled,
    snow-capped feeders.
        Could life possibly
        hold more beauty than this?

39.

February 15

heart of my heart

At the depth of my soul
is intimacy & shelter,
the hearth of the heart...
the flickering of the heart's fire
inviting me to come home
to my self...
the flames reflecting loving truths-
  "Your truest 'you' dwells here...
  You contain God as God contains you...
  Rest & be blessed...
  Come back always to the heart space..."

Realization dawns as
the light enlightens-
  I cannot see what
  lies beyond my reach...
  I can only feel connections
  of the heart...
    HEART/HEARTH
    SOUL/SOLITUDE
    BLESSED/BLESSING
    REST/RESTORATION

If you want the truth,
I will tell you the truth:
Friend, listen: the God
whom I love is inside.
                -Kabir

I greet all that dwells within,
finding not perfection but peace...
            welcome
            inclusion
            acceptance.

And again the Spirit sings,
  "In your hearts's space,
  you are as you are to be...
  always, ever growing, changing...
  fluid, flexible, not tied down,
            not spelled out.
            Enter often."

February 16

my muse

The Muse begins
to return, to rise from
her dormancy to stalk
through my life, demanding
my attention, demanding
to be heard.
She is fearsome!
will brook no cowardice, no
procrastination on my part.
I hear her shouting...
    singing...
    see her stomping...
    dancing along the
    corridors of my life.
At sixty-six, I feel in
some ways that my life is
just beginning...
that I am emerging newborn
into the creative life,
  the writing life,
     midwived into being
     by the pushy, persistent
     Muse who will not
       let me go.

February 17

My youngest sister, Rennie, was born on this day. She died in an auto accident on Christmas Eve when she was twenty-five and never does her birthday pass without my wondering what she would be like here & now... at this age and time. I miss her still.

com-passion

There are days, like
today, when I need
someone to "compassion" me...

to suffer with me...
to walk the difficult &
   darkening path, simply
   holding my hand.

Caught up in a maelstrom of emotions,
shaken by the intensity of long-buried
feelings, plunged into the depths
of despair, how it helps to have a hand
to hold tightly...
      and a voice to say
      again & again,
         "No, you're not crazy.
         Let your tears flow.
         They won't wash you
         away. The darkness
         will not blind or bind
         you. I am here-
         you are not walking
            this way alone."

February 18

A good traveler has no fixed plans and is not intent on arriving.
-Tao Te Ching

the road

The Beatles sang
about the path of life-
   "The Long and Winding Road"
   they called it...
         fitting words to
         bring to mind the
         path we travel
            day by day...

Neither the beginning nor
the ending is in sight,
for though each of us is
born, the memory of that
passage into life is lost
   in infancy's forgetfulness...

though each of us will
die, the knowledge of the
day & time is blessedly
beyond our ken,
    hidden in the shadows
    of what-is-yet-to-be.

And so I walk the road
on which I find myself
today- step by step I go...
   one foot in front of another...
      sometimes stumbling,
      sometimes skipping in
         joyful abandon,
      but always hand in hand
      with the God Who Comes...
        whoever She is...
        however He is revealed.

February 19

We are not
Over
When we think
We are.
      -Alice Walker

trees in winter
Winter is so lovely...
bare & stark, nature
pared down to its simplest, truest self.
Branches stripped of leaves stand
in naked beauty against the
blue-gray sky...
   aging women stripped
   of pretentions or artifice
   to stand proudly, defiantly
   before the winter wind,
      patiently awaiting the blooming
      springtime when, once again,
      they will be clothed in
      nature's colorful finery...

but, for now,
    reveling in naked freedom
    and waving their arms
    in joyous, shivering
            abandon.

February 20

apart...
I feel a part...
I feel apart...
        the story of
        so much of
        my life.
A part of the church...
apart from the polity...
            the rules...
            the "party line"...
A part of this nation...
 apart from the politics...
                the in-fighting...
                the power struggles...
                the war...
A part of my family...
apart from the grudges...
            the squabbling- most often unspoken...
            the misunderstandings...
            the hurts- deliberate or unintentional...
A part of my gender...
apart from the pettiness...
            the incessant drive for outer beauty...
            the need for male approval...
Is it any wonder
that sometimes
I feel I am
f
    a ll
        ing
            to   p   ie   ce   s?
44.

February 21

Your face is a mirror of your life- every bit of your history is etched there. And your body holds all of the memories you have made- good, bad, indifferent. Why in the world would you ever want to deny such a gift?

aging with grace

What is this persistent emphasis
   on looking young?
What's wrong with aging?

Why can't we older women
   recognize & celebrate that
   we are examples, mentors
   for the young? that *how*
   we age, *how* we live out our
   years will open the eyes & minds
     & hearts of younger women to
     the holiness & gifts of aging
          wisely & well?

So – STOP complaining about
         your weight…
         your hair…
         your wrinkles…
         your shape…
They are part of WHO YOU ARE!!!
   And that you is beautiful!
         amazing!
         full of knowledge &
           experience!
         alive with possibility &
           buoyed by the memory
           of triumph over adversity!

Celebrate yourself today-
   your aging, lovely, incredible
         self!

We turn not older with years, but newer every day. -**Emily Dickinson**

February 22

Though I usually lay claim to the name 'Christian', a more accurate descriptive term would be 'believer'- at least most of the time. And I have long been engaged in a love/hate relationship with the Church, as I continually wrestle with creeds and dogma and theology and orthodoxy which does not resonate with my heart & mind.

CREDO...
Be with me today,
  Spirit of Christ.
You know of my
  struggles with
  the Church...
   with its doctrine and theology...
   with a cosmology too
    narrow and exclusive
    for my heart and life.
Help me to speak
  this struggle...
  to make sense of it...
  to share it...
   I know You...
   I don't know You.
Or help me to let go of
  the struggle and
   just BE...
let me dwell in hope
  and the affirmation
  that, within all of life,
   there IS meaning and
   purpose-
    for me
    for the world
and that You- whoever
  You are- undergird
    bear up
    in-fill all of it.
For this day,
  at this moment,
   this is my statement of faith-
    and IT IS ENOUGH.

At the place of faith, I'm not sure that I'm sure.
-Richard Rohr

46.

February 23

I am awash in the news of the day, for better or worse, and I find I cannot ignore it- yet am unsure what to do about it. Perhaps at this moment in time I am being called to be a 'witness'...to attend to and care for the wounds of the world, as best I can, even if it is only with my attention and concern. Perhaps, as I allow myself to be immersed in it all, direction will come.

reality

Around me swirls the
rhetoric of presidential politics...
    and I am hit between the
    eyes by yet another foul ball
    tossed by an administration
    whose policies I abhor.

I hear the doleful warnings
of environmental scientists...
    and I am stuck in the
    quagmire of the realities of
    global warming and our collective
    refusal to make responsible change.

I listen to the news of
economic instability as
    round the world, business interests &
    spending take center stage,
    shoving poverty & need into
    the wings to languish unseen.

And I realize that, try as I might
to avoid & evade, I am being called
to engage in a lovers' quarrel
with the world in which
I live...
    but how do I begin?
    And where, oh where,
        am I headed?

Our lives extend beyond our skins, in radical interdependence with the rest of the world. -Joanna Macy

February 24

We are caught in an inescapable network of mutuality, tied in a single garment of destiny. Whatever affects one directly affects all indirectly.
-Martin Luther King, Jr.

enough...

"Enough is enough!"
an old expression of
exasperation, uttered
by someone at the end
of his rope, at the limit
of her endurance.
"No more!" it said...
"Halt!"..."Stop..." whatever
was causing pain or anger,
consternation or confusion.
"Enough is enough!"-
drawing a line...
setting a limit...
   "I will take no more,"
   the words implied...
         no more sass...
         no more abuse...
         no more excuses...
            NO MORE!
But perhaps- just perhaps-
these words require another
look...a turn of the kaleidescope
of perception to see them in
a new way...
   an affirmation of the
   abundance of my life...
   for I truly <u>have enough</u>-
       enough food to keep me fed & healthy...
       enough money to meet my needs...
       enough love from family & friends...
       enough of *everything,* including talents &
         abilities, to make life
           full & rich & satisfying.
What do I lack? NOTHING...so
            enough IS enough!

February 25

This was written for my son, Paul, on his birthday. The word describes him so well: a big, tall, big-hearted young man with a hearty laugh who tries to meet the world with a wide open spirit and an often-child-like trust...or perhaps it describes the man I wish & hope he can become.

mensch
Isn't that a glorious word?
Yiddish, you know, the name
for one who lives from
      the heart...
          fully & completely...
whose every action comes from
a deep inner well of caring &
      enthusiastic love for
      all creatures, for
        all creation.
I picture Tevya,
fiddling on the roof-
or Zorba, dancing
in the street-
or Jesus, risking everything
    to reach out to the very ones
    the world had tossed aside...
or Rosa Parks, resting tired
    body seated on the bus,
    setting a nation on
    its ear, and shattering
    the status quo.

February 26

I gave birth to these words on the anniversary of the death of my eldest son, Carl. The death of a child, regardless of his or her age, forever changes you. And though time passes, though the pain lessens, the experience of grief, the sense of loss, never truly ends.

birthing grief
Loss happens in this life...
loss happens and we need to
give birth to grief...allow all of
the feelings to come to light...to life...

But too often we abort the birthing...
and our grief is stillborn-
   never finding expression-
or miscarried-
   expressed inadequately & incompletely
And so the grief-not-expressed
goes somewhere else...
that complex plethora of
responses & emotions not allowed
to come to life takes residence
somewhere within us...
   becomes parasitic,
   drawing life & strength
   from body & soul,
   sapping strength & health,
        joy & meaning.
So- how many live with
a heavy heart? with something
eating away at them?
How many need to get
something off their chest?
live with a vague, gut-wrenching
sense of something
        out of kilter?
Grief, perhaps, crying out to
be heard...to be given life &
expression...to be acknowledged
        and lived through.
The reality is- **grief hurts!**
hurts dreadfully! and to birth
it into being means
        we will hurt!
       Birthing always does...
       but in embracing the pain...
       in going with it, instead
       of fighting against it,
           we let it- and so ourselves-
           become a living, breathing
           reality...a reality in which
           growth & learning & strengthening
              can take place.

The bad news-
  it may take a
  very long time.
The good news-
  we will walk out on the
  other side healed...re-born...
            a new person...
            re-shaped, to be sure,
                but ALIVE!
                FULLY ALIVE!

*There is a strength learned from suffering that cannot be learned
any other way.* -**Matthew Fox**

February 27
*Usually sleep comes easily to me...but there are times when unbidden painful
memories flood my mind and heart and sleep eludes me in the deluge of
feelings, the flood of emotions.*

insomnia
I lay upon my bed, unsleeping...
filled with unshed tears...
          unspoken pain...
          unuttered anguish
              rending the fabric of my heart and
              rendering me broken-hearted...
And so I shrieked a voiceless
cry of help..."Hold me, Mother God!
Cradle me, Brother Christ!
   Gather me in loving arms...
   soothe my aching heart &
   mind...lift me from this darkness..."
And as the warmth surrounded
me, the sense of Presence,
real & strong, I cried...and slept...
and woke refreshed, renewed
          to face another day...
              thankful to be alive.

February 28

This poem owes its inspiration to the writings of Ted Loder, whose words & expressions always poke and prod me, whose creative imagination takes my breath away. The lovely expression, 'cosmic homesickness', is his creation.

seeking

'Cosmic homesickness'...
I read these words
again & yet again,
convinced that they describe
the state of every searching heart...
a longing, irrepressible & deep,
for something which we cannot name
    but which we miss...
a sense of deprivation welling
    from our very core...
a yearning for transcendence,
    for something *more* than
    ordinary life...
      and so we search & seek...
          we read & study...
          we travel- at least in the
              mind's eye- to places
                far & wide...
      only to find, after all our journeys,
      all our struggle, all our questioning
      & inquiry, that we have arrived at
      the threshold of our own heart...
      and opening the door, we find the very
      thing for which we sought-
          the Presence of
          the One Who Loves
          sitting on the couch
          with arms open wide.

> *We shall not cease from exploration*
> *And the end of all our exploring*
> *Will be to arrive where we started*
> *And know the place for the first time.* -T.S. Eliot

February 29 - Leap Year Day

incongruous
Four more closets
cleaned & organized...
twelve full bags of
"stuff" I no longer need
offered up to those
            who do...
a bag of books donated
to the library...
paring life down to
reasonable size...
focusing on "less" instead
            of "more"...
        on "need" instead
            of "want"...
A breath of fresh & holy air
wafts through my life
as I let go of "having" to
focus on "giving"...
            and then I tune in to
            NPR and listen to authoritative
            voices say that lowering the
            interest rates will help the
            economy by making it
            easier to borrow...to be drawn
        more deeply into debt's
            deceptive maelstrom- where far
            too many of us already dwell,
            tempest-tossed...
Now, here I sit, pulled asunder
by the inconsistencies of
what I hear & what I know...
            Lord, have mercy.

reflections...

MARCH -
spring approaches

March 1

I am a part and parcel of the whole, and I cannot find God apart from the rest of humanity. -**Mahatma Gandhi**

one

To be "centered"
does not mean
to be "closed"...
to go to the core of
one's own self is to
recognize, acknowledge
that *every* person has
      a "core"...
      an inner depth
      where dwells the
      truest self...
      that self who each
      of us is meant to be...
        and yours will not
        look like mine...
            or hers...
            or his...
      for in the celebration of
      uniqueness that is
      humanity, there are
      a million million selves
      that seek expression,
      that struggle to be born,
      that long to see the light of day...

And so, perhaps, the holy path,
the sacred calling is to see...
           accept...
           affirm...
the divinity inherent in each one
    who shares this
    life & time...
        to acknowledge and to name them
        "sister", "brother"...members of
        one family of humankind.

56.

March 2

*The spiritual life does not come cheap. It is not a stroll down
a Mary Poppins path with a candystore God who gives sweets
and miracles. It is a walk into the dark with the God who is the light
that leads us through the darkness.* **-Joan Chittister**

fear & faith

Denial of fear & pain in
the name of faith is
denial of one's truest,
deepest self...denial of
one's humanity. For
how does our faith
grow if never challenged
by the circumstances,
the totality of life? How
can one live in true
relationship with the
Divine without questions,
without doubts? Faith is
not, after all, getting rid
of or denying fear-
it is facing it,
learning to
name it,
walking through it-
            and emerging on the
            other side WHOLE...
            battered & scarred,
                    but WHOLE.

March 3

*It is hard to seize a disturbing truth when a comfortable life
depends on toning it down.* **-Arthur Simon**

just asking...

Okay, God,
so this is how it is...
I have to come clean,
        to be genuinely, authentically
        truthful with you-

and with myself...
I do not have a clue
about what you want from me-
> how I am to live...
> how I am to be faithful & faith-filled...
I mean, I *say* the right
things about caring about the poor,
> about wanting justice & peace
> in this world...
I inform myself & pray & give money...
> but does this really matter?
> Or are the only ones who make
> a difference those who
> dedicate their lives- their *LIVES*-
> to *doing* what needs to be done...
>> working in clinics in Haiti
>> bringing food to refugees in Kenya
>> caring for orphans in Bosnia
>> comforting the sick in the streets of Calcutta
>> lobbying for justice for immigrants &
>> illegal aliens in this country
I like to convince myself that
I *am* doing my part by
being faithful where I am,
living consciously & conscientiously...
> after all, writing & preaching & teaching...
> being a caring daughter & mother &
> grandmother & friend & pastor
>> are all important work...
>> make the world a better place...
>> or so I tell myself...
>>> But is it true? Or is it simply
>>> another way of letting myself
>>> off the hook of *living* my faith?
>>> I don't know...
>>> I'm just asking...
>>> and wondering...
>>>> Amen

March 4

courage
this is courage:
   to face your inner conflicts & fears
   to acknowledge your longing
      for security & approval,
   yet to remain on the path
      you believe is the right one
      for you...
         in spite of the difficulty
         in spite of your vulnerability
         in spite of the disapproval or
           misunderstanding of others...
   to live this way
   makes you a hero...
      one with the courage to BE.

March 5
When we find our own music, sing our own song, give of ourselves completely to others or to our work and our passions, we are acknowledging the great gift of existence and saying thank you. **-Alan Jones**

my song
I have a song
to sing...
   sometimes it flows
   in joyful abandon,
   emerging without
   effort or deliberation
      notes both pure & true,
      soaring like the voice of
         violin or flute into the
         day's glorious brightness.

And when the skies are gray,
when gloom o'ertakes me,
   then my song takes on
      the dirge-like tones
         of cello or bassoon...
      resonant & deep,

yet lovely still...
filling out the
orchestral symphony
        that is my song...
                my life.

March 6

One thing I have learned over the years: we each grieve in our own way. And it is important that I do not judge the path of another as I am not walking in her shoes; I am not feeling his pain. The ways in which my children & I coped after the death of my husband, their dad, may have seemed strange to some, but we walked the path we had to walk...and I suspect that my adult children are walking it still.

grief work

Moving into uncharted
territory...going where
you have never gone
before...this is part of
becoming who you are
meant to be...
        self-actualization, some
        call it, though such a
        formal-sounding term
        cannot begin to hold
        the truth of daring and
        derring-do which meeting
        life head-on requires...

I remember driving
country roads on Sunday
afternoons with the children
after their dad, my husband,
died, pausing at each crossroads
to ask, "Which way?"- then
turning at their bidding,
together moving into the
uncharted territory of grief,
discovering who we now
were as a family...
overcoming our collective fear

by daring to take an unfamiliar
road, confident- as I told the
children- that all the roads
would eventually take
us home.

   We *had* to dare, it seemed...
   to take the risk of going
   to where life had already
   taken us...but this time,
   to *choose*...

   *Through remembering we discover that any present dilemma is not
   disconnected from what has happened before, and that the God who saw
   us through past tragedies will see us through our present difficulties.
   Through remembering we take the broken or wrongly assembled jigsaw
   of our lives and discern our proper pattern. But it takes time.*
   -John L. Bell

March 7

*Sometimes a change of perspective is exactly what we need to stir gratitude
for life within us...to open our eyes to the beauty and glory of each day. On
this morning, I gazed out of the window of a lovely B&B in Wilmington, North
Carolina, as I looked forward to spending the day with my daughter, Hope.*

another day (in Wilmington)

The sun has not yet risen
and the sky is gray with clouds,
but outside my borrowed
window stands- no, dances-
a glorious tulip magnolia,
the cups of white and pink
of every shade rising skyward,
open to the many blessings &
wonders of the day, certain they
will come, certain life will continue,
certain God is good...while I sit here
before the fire, with pen in my
hand and coffee from another's
serving hand nearby, filled with
wonder at the faithful presence
that I see, determined to begin

my day with face & arms lifted
heavenward as well, open to receive
the gifts & mysteries that simply living
will bestow this day.
Grant me, Beloved Spirit,
the faith of the magnolia,
that I might stand as firm & lovely
in the presence of this life
I have been given
                    - today.

March 8 - International Women's Day

Am I a feminist? Most assuredly...for I claim and celebrate the feminine in me, in all of us, as a gift this world most desperately needs.

the FEMININE

The FEMININE:
   recognizing & honoring
   the creative
        cherishing
        nurturing
        mystical side of one's personality...
that part of ourselves which
  is drawn toward light & color
                     darkness & texture
                     candlelight & velvet
                     the beauty of ritual & liturgy
                     the resonant sound of drumming
                     the airy phrases of Mozart
                     the picture language of Mary Oliver...
that part of ourselves
   which accepts questions &
        does not demand answers...
   which sees life as an
        unfolding, blooming process of
        ongoing cycles...ever new
                     ever renewing
                     ever alive with
                          possibility...

62.

March 9

*Learn to be quiet enough to hear the sound of the genuine within
yourself so that you can hear it in others.*
-Marian Wright Edelman

advice

When we give advice,
aren't we failing
to believe in the intrinsic
    wisdom of the other?
to trust that the Inner
    Teacher which resides
    within each one of us
    will lead & guide?
to believe & respect that
    other one to work on
    his own journey? walk
    her own path?
Advice, I think, should
not be an unsolicited
"gift", but only sought-after
wisdom, given with fear &
trembling & humility...a
hand, reached out in
loving & compassionate
response...an RSVP to
the invitation to walk
together for a time on
the journey we call Life.

March 10

Written for my beautiful second son, Mark, who will understand.

crazy...

Once upon a time- and
perhaps that one time
is even now in places
far away from here-
    people who saw visions
    or heard voices were
    considered to be holy...

touched by the divine...
and so, revered,
      respected,
      cared for, and
      protected
by the community
they touched.

> *To what end were*
> *we oddballs born?*
> **-Annie Dillard**

But here & now in this
world built on intellect
and reason, we look on
any inner turmoil as
needing treatment
rather than encouragement...
    the one whose ears hear
    drumbeats unheard by
    all the rest is diagnosed
    and classified, while
    protection is reserved
    for all the rest of us as
    we turn away from the
    person dancing to the beat
          or
stomping through puddles
in order to see the rainbows
created by the sun upon
the water droplets...
    and sighing, "Beautiful!
        Beautiful!"

reflections...

March 11

inner life

Your inner life is the
source of what manifests
in your outer life...
So-
      BE peace
      BE joy
      BE courage
      BE creativity
      BE truth
      BE trust
      BE possibility
Nothing has to *happen*
for you to live fully-
        JUST DO IT!
        Yes, you can.

March 12

at arm's length

We hold death at
arm's length- or so
we think-
when, in reality,
we are living in
its midst at every moment.

reflections...

March 13
*I am seldom really sick but late this winter- just as spring was arriving, in fact-
I was struck by a nasty virus...the flu, perhaps, but whatever it was called, it
laid me low and all I could do was give it full rein and permit my body to heal
itself.*

body language
I feel lousy.
No pretty words
to dress up just how
dreadfully sick I feel.
Pounding head, burning
eyes, aching throat...
and exhaustion!
The sense of slogging
through a hundred
miles of mud & muck,
a heavy pack upon my
back...with no relief
in sight. Energy depleted...
sinuses clogged...the flow
of life itself is blocked...
> Grant an opening,
> Healing Spirit...of what is
> closed & clogged...an opening
> in my understanding...
> a window in my heart & soul
> to admit healing light...to permit
> the pent up spirit of illness to
> escape...
The body needs what
the body needs...
> time
> rest
> comfort
> patience...
> and my own loving
care...and wholeness
> will happen once again.
> > Let it be so.

March 14

How we see and what we see changes even as we change the lens through which we behold the world around us, and making a turn of the kaleidescope of our gaze gives us a whole new perspective.

in-between

When I look down, I see
blooming spring...
    crocuses and daffodils
    abound, snowdrops nod
    their gentle heads, and
    pansies left from fall's
    last planting lift their
    charming faces
    to the nurturing sun.

When I look up, I see
stark winter's barrenness...
    trees stripped bare of
    leaf & fruit, not yet
    budded green but waiting,
    as if with bated breath, to
    play their part in Nature's
    riotous symphony.

I am experiencing schizo-vision,
    as I gaze at this time
    in-between, this still-winter,
    not-quite springtime...
    the already & not yet
    push-pull of life playing
    itself out in living color
    and black-and-white
    before my eyes.

March 15

*We're told as children- even as adults- to 'play by the rules'. Whether I do or not really depends for me on **what** the 'rules' are and **whose** they are.*

some rules...

Not fond of 'rules'...
though as guidelines for
behavior, they serve a
useful purpose, I guess...
   so here are some
   I have come to trust-

- Don't say YES when you feel NO.
- We cannot change anyone else.
- Trust people enough to share the true you.
- Get out of your own way!
- It is not loving to help yourself get hurt.
- Without passion, life is failed magic.
- Purpose is formed in solitude, but lived in community.
- Be careful not to imprison yourself in the opinions of others.
- We love best from a sense of overflow.
- Not forgiving ourselves makes us afraid to risk, create, or feel.
- Embody what you say you believe.
- Setting free your gifts is the essential labor of life.
- Trouble comes to *pass,* not to stay.

You're welcome to them
if they speak *your* truth...
for, believe me, few are writ
in stone, and so will change
as I live out my days...
      so much for "rules".

March 16

The people who help us grow toward true self offer unconditional love, neither judging us to be deficient nor trying to force us to change but accepting us exactly as we are. –**Parker Palmer**

helpful

what does it mean to
be helpful? there is an
eternal rhythm to life
which we must honor, to
which we must pay heed...
    most people respond,
    come to life, in their own
    way, in their own time,
    and perhaps, if we try to
    hasten the process, we do
    harm...perhaps in our intent
    to be helpful, we are doing
    subtle violence to each other...
    perhaps our greatest gift is to
    offer our confidence in the process
    of life working out in another...
which does not mean walking away
in unconcern, but rather standing
watchfully on the borders of their
personhood, trusting that they
have *within themselves* whatever
resources they need...neither
invading nor evading but staying
present-
    without trying to *fix.*
to help is not to direct
outcomes for another, not
to solve their problems, but
to honor the soul...
    opening the door to integrity...
    creating a circle of trust...
it is a "yes, you can"..."i have
faith in you" kind of support...
        it is LOVE.

March 17

Je ne regrette rien.
-Edith Piaf

regret
Is it possible, I wonder,
to live life without Regret—
to actually come to
the place of wisdom
where all you see are
the building blocks of
                your life...
        event upon event
        choice upon choice
        forming the person
        you have become...
        the person you are now...
living into, celebrating the certain
awareness that without
        each one of them—
        each stumbling block
        each road not taken
        each difficult & dangerous
                        choice
you would not
        be YOU...
        but someone else
                entirely.

So embrace her—
this You you have become—
hold her tenderly and
close the door of
your heart on
        Regret.

March 18

the birds
The birds sang
   before dawn today...
      hope in the darkness...
      confidence in the rising of the sun...
      no concern about
         what will happen...
      just being all they were
         created to be.
No wonder Jesus said,
"Regard the birds...
pay attention to them...
learn from them."
   And so my day begins...

March 19
These words were written on March 19, 2008, the fifth anniversary of the war in Iraq.

five years...and counting
Five long years...
one thousand eight hundred twenty-seven days...
countless thousands of lives lost...
thousands more changed
   forever in ways we cannot
   even imagine by head injuries
   and lost limbs...by "post-
   traumatic stress disorder"-
      and even our language has changed,
      as "disorder" cannot begin to describe
      a life forever misshaped by the horrors
      seen & experienced...
families destroyed- here and
in Iraq...children without parents...
parents losing children...husbands,
wives ripped away... all in the
name of- what?
         Power?

Domination?
Oil?
Our American appetite for it continues insatiable...
and we dare descry the loss of our
"American way of life" as the
stock market plunges & banks
close & property values plummet &
jobs are lost...while on distant
shores, a "way of life" has been
held in abeyance for five long
years.
        Lord, have mercy.

And our government continues
to speak of "Iraqi freedom"...but
surely it cannot be about freedom,
since in this dreadful "War on Terror"
we have lost so much of ours...allowing
it to slip through our fingers like sand
on the Iraqi desert...since our government
keeps "terror" alive within American
hearts & minds to justify, to gain
support for, this oxymoronic war-
   which is destroying us
   as surely as it is
   destroying the Iraqi people.
        Lord, have mercy.

Five long years...
one thousand eight hundred twenty-seven days...
and- irony of ironies- we stand here in the middle of
Holy Week...
   commemorating the unholy
   slaying of the man called Jesus
   by the powers of his day...
   commemorating the unholy
   slaughter of peace and justice
   by the powers of our day.
        Lord, have mercy.

Fall to your knees, friends & foes,
Red states & Blue...

hang heads in shame for what
we have permitted in *our name*...
   then rise up with a mighty
   "No more!" resounding...
         No more war!
         No more fear!
         No more lives for oil!

BE the peace for which
   you long!
BE the hope for which
   our nation craves!
BE the loving compassion
   which is the path
   to justice this world
   needs!
                  Lord, have mercy,
                  and strengthen us
                  to live the truth.
                     Amen & amen

No war can be long carried on against the will of the people.
-Edmund Burke

March 20
I had participated in my first peace rally; and it was Maundy Thursday, in the midst of what the Church calls 'Holy Week' and the ironies of existence were right there in front of me.

firsts
Yesterday, my first public peace rally!
In the wind and rain with others who
have done this many times before...
hearts & minds united in the cause of peace.

Today, another first- the first day of spring...
and outside, the birds are serenading the day,
as if they know, adding their accompaniment
to the strains of the lovely "Romance" by
Shostakovich wafting through the air of my
room...sublime creations, both...from the hand

of the Creator, from the hand of a created
co-creator...
Today, tonight, we commemorate
that meal shared by a group of disciples,
friends, that binds millions of us
together to this day...yet which can
also separate & divide...can tragically
exclude...when its intent has always been,
I think, to unite, to lift up, to convey love &
acceptance, forgiveness & welcome...begun,
according to tradition & story, by the one
who showed, taught, *lived* the very nature of God...
and who said, "Regard the birds..."
   "Don't worry," he was saying...
   "Trust in the love & compassion
   of God...in and around you...
   and as you are filled, so you
   can fill the world."

Outside, the wind breathes heavily through
the trees...the sky has lightened, but no sign
of the sun as yet...and a veritable symphony
of birdsong conveys the message to this often
heart-weary pilgrim: "Trust and believe.
   Hold hope as a precious living reality.
   At the deepest level, you can find peace,
   even when all around you seems to belie it."

And the words of another long-ago pilgrim
ring in the ears of my heart...
   "All shall be well, and all shall be well,
   and all manner of thing shall be well."
   the words of Julian ringing across
   seven centuries to comfort, to
   bring hope, to unite hearts &
   minds & lives on this Maundy Thursday...
   on this first day of spring...
   on this first day of the
      sixth year of the war in Iraq...
         Hope springs...tears flow...
         hope springs...welcome, Spring.
74.

March 21

*In violence we forget
who we are.*
-Mary McCarthy

war & peace
Warring forces, threatening to
tear your self apart...pulled
first this way & then that,
the self crying out for truce...
a cessation of the inner violence
tearing limb from limb, body
from soul, mind from heart.
Perhaps it is time- high time-
to declare a moratorium...
become a conscientious
objector to what puts us at war
with ourselves...the competing
demands on time, attention,
compassion, love; the causes-
good & worthy, every one- which
cry out for our life's blood; the
people who want more & more
of us until the inner well runs
dry, with nothing left to give.
    So wave the white flag.
    Put your arms to rest.
    Stage a sit-in with yourself on
        a bench outdoors amidst the
        blooming beauty of today.
                And breathe. Smile. Welcome peace.

March 22

sick to death...
"I am sick to death of it..."
an expression we use...
    SICK TO DEATH...
though we don't mean it
literally, do we? not really...

But what about when life has no
meaning, but death is too frightening?
Then those hurting ones become
            the walking wounded...
            the living dead...
            like the old horror movie,
                "Night of the Living Dead"...

Have you ever felt like that?
Well, I have...unable to see the light...
life one long, dark night...
feeling more dead than alive.
    But NO ONE KNEW!
How could I be walking around
bleeding...totally dis-membered...
    and NO ONE KNOW?

Why did no one else know I was
coming apart?
Was I totally invisible?
Or did I do such a good job of
covering up my wounds?
    and WHY did I?

Because people were depending on me
    to help *them*...to heal *them*...
and after all, no one wants their 'savior' to
be wounded...to be hurting...and if they are-
    well tough! Suck it up!
    I want you to tend to *my* wounds, they say...
                take care of *me*...

Perhaps that's why so many people
avoid church on Good Friday...*their*
'savior' isn't supposed to bleed & die...
isn't supposed to cry out in pain...
isn't supposed to feel forsaken.
So let's run past the ugly cross
with its pain & suffering...let's
run to glory!
    to sunlight!
    to triumph!

But the truth is, the hard truth,
the dark, painful truth,
the walking-through-the-fire truth-
  you have to die
  before you can be
  resurrected...
  re-born...
   and I am sick to death.

Tell all the Truth but tell it slant.
-Emily Dickinson

March 23

early spring
Nearly seven and still dark;
bits of light are diluting
the darkness but daylight
seems very far away.
Oh! There, in that corner
windowpane, I see a
lightening of the darkness,
in the space of just a few moments...
the legerdemain of sunrise...
day calling, day beginning,
   ready or not!

March 24
 *One's life becomes a brightly woven cord of mindfulness that weaves
through the ordinarily mundane dimension of living and imbues it with
a sacred dimension.* **-Frank MacEowen**

good morning
Outside my window
the Japanese maple
is greening...her
delicate branches
shivering in the March
wind and aglitter with
the remaining gems of

nightime rain...
my constant, silent,
faithful companion,
arms spread wide
in welcome...her
hospitality reaching out
to birds, to squirrels,
to sun & rain, to
the human who sits
near enough to
touch & be enfolded
by her...
Soon her canopy
will enshroud me
each morning as
I sit amidst her
branches to read &
write & rejoice in
the gift of
     another day.

March 25

Good health is such a gift. Often I take it for granted, though less so as I get older. And wellness involves not only body but also mind and spirit- the whole person, the person wholly holy.

wellness

Wellness is a gift, a grace, a warm blanket
    wrapping body & soul
    against the slings & arrows
    of outrageous fortune.
Wellness is a joy, a state of inner peace,
    a blissed & blessed
    place of ease in which the
    heart finds its rest.
Wellness lives in hope...lives out of hope...
    breathes a sigh of
    contentment on a weary soul,
    affirming all is well.
        Today, I thank God I am well...

March 26

With the spring comes the memory of my dad's death...a larger-than-life man who impacted everyone who knew him, and left a lasting legacy of love & laughter for his family.

lamentation

Death is the great unequalizer...
when one you love
has died,
    disorientation sets in...
    disequilibrium...
the shape of life
is shape no more...
    a cacophony of thought &
    spirit reigns...
Where boundaries once were,
    none remain...
        only a blurry landscape
        in which every step is
        taken as if walking blind...
And even the shape
of who you were- before-
    is formless, now,
    and undefined...
The face that looks back
from the mirror,
    a stranger...

Who am I, you wonder...
what is my place?
    and how, oh how,
    will I survive
        today?

reflections...

March 27

Hatred will never cease by hatred.
By love alone it is healed.
-The Buddha

terrorism
When you are
   abjectly poor,
when you live
   without hope,
when you see others
   with so much,
   while you have so
     little,
what do you
have to lose by
   becoming a terrorist?
       a suicide bomber?

Why is it so difficult
for us as a nation- as a people-
   with so many "haves"
   among the world's "have-nots"-
     to recognize
       acknowledge
         our complicity
         in a worldview
         which makes terrorism
         not only possible but
         inevitable?

For when hope is gone,
   what rushes in to
   fill the nature-abhorred
   vacuum?
       fear
       anger
       the need for retribution,
       real or imagined.
         Lord, have mercy.

80.

March 28

The goal of all spirituality is that in the end the naked person stands before the naked God. -**Richard Rohr**

truth

How did we ever get the idea
that the spiritual life
is about DESTINATION?
The spiritual life is PROCESS
                JOURNEY
                PILGRIMAGE
                TRANSFORMATIVE EXPERIENCE...
It is the here & now magnificence
                and minutiae of life...
        the here & now suffering
                and sublimity of living...
Spiritual truths are spoken
in a variety of languages...
saying the same things in
        different words...
    telling the same truths using
        different stories...
    painting a variety of signposts
        to leave along the path, hoping
        they may provide guidance
            to another-
    yet always aware that every
    "other" has to find her own way...
        discover his own path...
    no "one size fits all" when it
        comes to the Spirit...
So why does so much of
religion insist on that?
            uniformity?
            conformity?
            adhering to the "party line"?
For who can deny
    my experience of
        the Divine? or yours?
    and who can control
            God's own Spirit?

March 29

Where a friendship recognizes itself as gift, it will remain open to its own ground of blessing. -John O'Donohue

the thread

Do you feel the connection?
that gossamer filament
that delicate thread
that shining web
    which holds us fast...
        heart to heart
        life to life?
Though I am here
and you are there...
    and there & there...
I feel your presence,
    here & now.
And even as my morning
coffee warms my body...
as the towhee & the robin
herald day's approach...
    I feel the warmth of *your*
        essential self filling &
        surrounding me...
    You are HERE-
        in some way I
        cannot explain
        but only feel...
you and every you
    who occupies and
    blesses my life...
        and I am filled...
            with joy
            with wonder
            with gratitude
        for this life-connection,
        this thread which
        holds us fast...
            heart to heart
            life to life.

March 30

*We must overcome the notion that we must be regular. It robs us
of the chance to be extraordinary and leads us to the mediocre.*
-Uta Hagen

daring poetry

Poetry is almost impossible
to define and I stand in awe
of those who dare it...
and since I am sometimes one
of them, ready to leap into   outer space
with no idea of where I will
land or how, I find I am on
occasion a daredevil, an
Evel Knievel of words, risking
life & limb to put my thoughts
on paper, uncertain of what
will happen to them-
            and to me...
Risky business, this wordsmithing...
risky, yet rewarding...in spite of
broken bones & broken hearts &
shattered dreams...hanging here in
seemingly-suspended animation
while flinging my words ahead
of me, trusting their landing
will cushion my own...
            but uncertain all the same...

March 31

holy presence

go deep
plunge deeper
let go-
    you will float
    on the waters of
    my Presence
be bathed in it
immerse yourself in it

let it cover & comfort you
let me bear you up
let me give you life
let my light guide you,
   my truth surround
            and fill you
there is nothing to fear
   and everything to gain
it is in the experience of Presence
   that you live
      in the reality that is God & good
               holy & just
this is a day of life-
      live every moment.

God hugs you. You are encircled by the arms of the mystery of God.
-Hildegard of Bingen

reflections...

APRIL-
spring has sprung

April 1

April Fool's Day, we call it...a day of practical jokes, silly puns, and laughter-not at all a bad thing. But this is also the first day of one of the loveliest months of the year, so why not enter it with a grateful and loving heart, with eyes wide open to the amazing landscape Nature paints? Why not make it a day to savor and celebrate just being alive?

morning psalm

I open my heart, Loving God...
I place myself in your hands...
I breathe in the beauty of
   the rising sun...
I savor the gift of another
   day of life...
Wherever this day leads,
   let me rest in the
   assurance of your presence
     with me
     in me
     under & around me...
Let me taste every moment
   and savor it all...
Hold me in your loving arms
   and breathe into me
   the blessing of peace...
Remove from my heart
   all fear
   all anxiety
   all that keeps me bound
     and threatens my freedom
        my growth...
For in you I find refuge...
   in you I find welcome...
   in you I find justice & hope...
   in you I find my fullest self...
     and IT IS ENOUGH.

April 2

*The precious promise of spring becomes especially poignant as time passes...
as the wisdom of aging makes me ever more aware that as each springtime
passes, its beauty must be appreciated, savored with gratitude and joy.*

tender spring

A tender spring...
   dogwoods, iris, violets, lilacs
      bloom, the breeze redolent with
      the scent of new life
            of beauty renewed...

And in this house,
   two aging women
   open doors & windows wide
      to welcome in the shining sun
            the life-scented air...

Together, they weave the
   tapestry of life with threads
      of love & hope
      of tears & laughter
      of energy & rest
      of tenderness & peace...
   aware that this shared path will
      someday end,
   and only one remain to
      savor the tender spring...
         So breathe hope!
           breathe joy!
           breathe love!
        Celebrate this day-
        and know-
               it is enough!

*The past is but the beginning of a beginning, and all that is and has been
is but the twilight of the dawn.* **-H.G. Wells**

April 3

mirror-image

When I look into the mirror,
I see the outer me-
    gray hair turning to white...
    graying, once-blue eyes..
    a sagging jawline & crepey neck...
    "laugh" lines around my
        eyes & mouth...
    and a body succumbing to
    the unfriendly pull
            of gravity.
My thighs have slid down
    to my knees and a once-flat
    stomach pouches out in
    defiance of my half-hearted
    efforts to hold it flat.
Once-lovely hands now
    show the thinning skin
    of age, while the lost
    subcutaneous fat, resulting
    in their wrinkled mein, has
    migrated to thighs & chin...
        impossible, I know, cold
        logic says, but there it is-
        and how do you argue with
        the mirror's truth?
And yet, inside, a girl remains-
young & fresh & full of joy...
lovely as a springtime day,
    fragrant & awash with light &
    flowers & the songs of birds...
        expectant
        hope-filled
        spilling over with the
        exuberance of youth...
        unlined, untainted by
        life's sorrows & demands...
So, which is the "real" me?
Or am I somehow truly both?

*I have walked through many
lives, some of them my own,
and I am not who I was,
though some principle of
being abides, from which I
struggle not to stray.*
           -Stanley Kunitz

A blend of past & present-
    aging crone
      AND
    youth-filled girl-
      in spite of what the mirror says.

April 4

Our flesh and blood, our body, is nothing but an envelope about our vital power. -Intinlik, Utkahakjaling Eskimo

placebo effect...

I heard a funny thing today
on NPR- or perhaps just a little
sad, perplexing and astonishing
at the same time...
a study done by students at MIT
to measure the effectiveness of
pain pills with the cost the
      only difference.
They- these students- "created"
a fake medication; wrote up a
brochure; even had pens made
with the name 'Belladone'
professionally printed, all to convince
      the subjects it was real.
But some of the pills were
listed at more than two dollars
each, while others were
discounted to ten cents-
and in the tests of response
to pain, the more expensive
pill worked with eighty-five percent
greater effectiveness, prompting
me to ask: Why was no one else
amazed at the apparent effectiveness of
a <u>made-up pill</u>?
  And what does this say about
  us and our bodies after all?

April 5

Prayer requests from dear friends had been coming in all week: Bonnie's son-in-law, Greg, facing his third major surgery for cancer; Diane's new granddaughter, Mackenzie, arriving too soon; families in turmoil and crisis needing loving support, needing healing and hope. And so I prayed...

morning prayer

Where is my heart at
this moment?
With the robin serenading the
not-yet-risen sun...
with the shared sublimity of
the music at last evening's
rehearsal...
with a tiny baby hanging
onto life in a Florida hospital...
with a determined young man
engaged in an on-going battle
with cancer...
with the elderly woman asleep
in her bed downstairs...
with my son on his way
to work, hoping for a better life...
with friends far & near, as
they rise & begin the choices &
struggles & joys of today...

Holy One, you who inhabit
my heart & mind & life,
   surround
   immerse
      every one of them- and me-
      in the blessing of love which
      never ends...which reaches
      out to comfort & connect...
      which is incarnate in our
      very human flesh.
         Amen & amen

...sitting in silence is to open the door to an authentic connection with God.
-Frank MacEowen

April 6

AFFIRMATION!
You are enough!
You are a human being
   worthy of respect!
         a created child of God...
         a unique creation of the Creator,
            made in the image of divinity...
            made to grab hold of, celebrate,
               your inestimable worth!
So- in your living-
   tell the truth- especially to yourself...
   be authentic in your choices...
   set boundaries- and remember- NO
      is a boundary...
   take time before responding
      to requests...
And the peace that passes
understanding will
pervade and energize
     your life!

April 7
*On some days we're left with looking at the world through
the lens of incoherence.* -**Barbara Hurd**

conundrum
It is a conundrum:
   how to live "small"-
     to care about
       cherish
       hallow the ordinary, every-day
             moments of life
     to honor
       love
       celebrate the family
            friends
           neighbors who
              populate my daily path-

while at the same time,
    to live **"big"**-
        to care about
           share responsibility
           work diligently
               for the well-being &
               healing of this world.

How do I- one small person,
    with one insignificant voice,
    make a difference?
        By doing <u>some</u> thing...
               <u>one</u> thing...
      by living fully...
           day by day...
               may it be enough.

April 8

The early morning is 'my' time. Rising between five and five-thirty, turning on my small coffee pot, putting my soft, blue prayer shawl around my neck, lighting a candle as I sit in a rattan chair, looking out of the window at the Japanese maple just outside, hearing the birds who welcome me into the day. This is my daily ritual, opening my heart to wherever it is being called, to whatever thoughts rise to the surface with the rising sun.

resurrection

Still dark...and so many approach the tomb
this day with heavy hearts,
with troubled spirits...
but many others, though bruised &
battered, near the grave with the
certainty that it will be empty...
death has come near but has retreated
    and their hearts are filled with the
    joyous song of Easter morn-
        "Risen! Risen! Risen!",
        ringing from Vivaldi's "Gloria",
        echoing from the cardinal & robin
        singing outside my window...
        resounding from my heart in
           life-giving affirmation...

in spite of the sadness
in spite of the fears
in spite of the waiting & wondering
wishing & praying
of the last few days.
I am borne on, surrounded by,
part of the wave of love & prayer
which has lifted up Amy & Greg,
Bonnie & Walt, John & Amber,
baby Makenzie throughout
these Three Days...

Now it is Easter morning, the Day of
Resurrection, and both Greg and baby
Mack are breathing on their own...their
lungs filled with the breath...
the spirit...
the wind of life...
hope fills & surrounds two families
today...making the new life of
the Day of Resurrection *real,*
perhaps as never before...
they have gone to the tomb
and found it empty- and Life-
for today- has triumphed!
Hallelujah!

Resurrection isn't just about life without end, but it's about life that begins now, eternally now. -**Ted Loder**

April 9

faith
Why do we so often speak of faith
as if it were a once and done thing-
instead of an ongoing,
dynamic process,
being shaped by our experiences...
by what we learn...by all we meet...
by everything which enters the arena
we call "life".

For just as I am not the same
small, blond child I once was,
    so my faith is not the same...
    has grown & changed, as living
    life has shaped me into someone
        very different than
        once I was so long ago.
And just as my reflection
in the mirror is unlike the
image there in years gone by,
    so the reflection of
    my faith has changed-
        and changes still-
            and will until
            the day I die.

Each of us is unfinished, a work in progress.
–Rachel Naomi Remen

April 10

violets

A carpet of purple
covers the side yard...
precious violet faces
peering from clusters of
heart-shaped green leaves...
    for such a brief spring time...
        and now a nosegay
        in a tiny vase graces
        my workspace, offering
        a blessing of Beauty & Love,
        reminding me that both
        are fleeting and yet
        eternal...
                yet another paradox
                of life's richness...
                another mystery to
                ponder & savor.

94.

April 11

friend to friend

A precious friend has shared
her fears, her need for presence,
for prayer. She has entrusted
herself into my hands, my heart...
and so here I am- fully present
                    fully prayerful
my love & intention & attention
directed to her need...to *her*...
Her healing- whatever that may be-
lies in other hands than mine...
but the heart she has entrusted
to me I hold gently but firmly in my
hands, cradling it with my own loving care.

Whether I feel worthy or not, I am
being the presence of God for her
right now, shining the light of Love
into her paralyzing darkness, using
my words to convey hope, to stir
courage, to provide a safety net
when the burden she is carrying
knocks her off the precarious path
she is traveling by necessity alone-
        but not unaccompanied.

Remember:
    Nothing is ever lost
    It is only
    Misplaced
    If we look
    We can find
    It
    Again
    Human
    Kindness.
        -Alice Walker

Love surrounds you, dear one...
cocoons you, cushions you,
comforts & protects you- not from
the storm itself, but from the
uncertainty, the loneliness of
walking this perilous road alone...
Rest in the certainty of being
companioned...breathe in the
holy peace of friendship & love...
and walk in the confident truth
that, no matter what happens,
'all manner of things shall be well.'

April 12

Being someone else is not what life is about. The question is,
How can I be me, fully me, truly me? The answer comes with great pain.
And the answer is, 'move on'.
-Joan Chittister

quiescence

A period of waiting often
   precedes growth...
a time of going deeper...
a time of learning to trust
   the inner self.
Rebirthing is painful...
   the labor of the new self
   emerging...
Growth's demands may
   cause temporary paralysis...
   produce seeming lethargy,
                  inactivity...
   make decision-making difficult
      as the body attempts to adjust to the
      desire, the call for
                  transformation...
      the nervous system exhausted
         and overtaxed...
            all the physiological dynamics
               of transcendence,
               of new growth,
               of rebirth.

April 13

dawn

Pink striations mark
   the site...
      the sun's path
      paved with beauty
            with glory...
A catch of breath-
   loveliness does that-
   reminds me that

life is holy...
creation is holy...
and, yes, I am holy...
The light-stained path
spreads out before me...
reminding me that
this life IS holy ground.
And I take off my shoes-
and DANCE!

Happiness is not a state to arrive at, but a manner of traveling.
-Margaret Lee Runbeck

April 14

stillness

The stillness of the early morning
breathes a blessing, a benediction
on my day. The darkness giving way to light...
the birthing of a new segment of living...
the awakening of a sleeping world...
of images of renewal,
rebirth,
resurrection.
The new life of a new day resonates
with hope...
with being given another chance.
No matter how much I blew it
yesterday, I am now being gifted
with a fresh opportunity-
to live fully
to exercise my creative muscles
to care *for* myself and
care *about* others
to express gratitude
to laugh & celebrate & rejoice
to deal with pain & sorrow
to BE the person I am created to be.
May today be a dancing day!
May it sing with joy & beauty & wonder!

April 15

Patience has never been my strong suit, but I find that as I age, the gift presents itself more and more frequently...and I am grateful.

patience

Patience is a choice...
to rely on the unceasing
movement of life...
to realize that things
will happen *when*
they happen...
to let go of insisting
on your own timetable...
to believe that what you
set in motion today
will have consequences,
bring about results-
> but who knows when?
Patience is making
time a friend instead
of seeing it as enemy...
savoring the possibilities...
experiencing the essence
   of each moment...
slowing down enough to
   come home to yourself...
realizing that your life is
   happening now...
and it is not a breathless
   race to an exhausted finish,
> but a gift- to be savored
> > cherished
> > appreciated
> > ## AT THIS VERY MOMENT!

Sometimes I sits and thinks
and sometimes I just sits.
-**Sachel Paige**

Sitting quietly
Doing nothing
Spring comes
And the grass
Grows
By itself. -**Basho**

April 16

daily prayer
Let the words of
        my mouth,
    the thoughts in
        my head,
    the actions of
        my body,
    the motivations of
        my heart,
            be true & loving &
            filled with the
            creative power of
            the Living Spirit
                this day.
And all manner –
    of things will be well...

April 17
The aim of life is not sameness, but variety...
the restlessness of transcendance, the adventure of novelty,
and rebellion against the status quo.
-Vaclav Havel

perfection
Perfectionism is the enemy!
Being perfect is a lie!
In the creative endeavor
that is life, we could *always*
do something better...
    but then nothing would
    ever be completed.
Imagine Van Gogh gazing
at his sublime "Starry Night"-
then adding just a few
    more daubs of paint...
or Beethoven, after completing
his magnificent "Fifth Symphony",
    tacking on just a few more notes.

Life is not about perfection
but wholeness...fullness...
        beauty...appreciation...
Focusing on the "if only" of
perfection narrows the mind,
pulls us out of the joy
        of the present.
After all, it's not about
"getting an A" from life-
        it is about learning & growing
                enjoying & appreciating...
        it is opening yourself to & celebrating
                the glory of imperfection.

April 18

change

Change comes...inevitably
                certain
    discomfitting us
    prodding us to alter our position
                to move
                to go in a different direction.
And like the children we once were,
    we cry out, "Why?"
                "It hurts!"
                "What will happen now?"
    clinging with clenched hands
        to the familiar
        the safe
        the what-once-was.
Why do we so easily forget that
only when we let go of the past,
the familiar, the safe, can new life happen?
                It's called RESURRECTION.

April 19

You do not have to be good.
You do not have to walk on your knees
for a hundred miles through the desert, repenting.
You only have to let the soft animal of your body
love what it loves.

-Mary Oliver

letting go

Can you change your plans
when life creates
    a different pattern?
Can you go with the flow
when the river of life
    encounters unexpected rapids?
Can you approach life
as a continuous melody
    rather than one note at a time?
I would like to think
I can answer an
unequivocal "YES" to
these queries...
        but that would be
        less than honest...
        as the part of me
        which craves order and
        control gives way
        only with great reluctance
        to the impatient,
                dancing child within.

April 20

My beautiful daughter's name is Hope- and so I dedicate this writing to her.

hope floats...

I believe that we are to be
not optimistic but hopeful.
Optimism too often sees
only the bright side- "every day
in every way we're getting better
and better"-

while Hope lights a candle
in the darkness.

Optimism accentuates the positive,
while often failing to recognize,
acknowledge the negative...
living with blinders on, in the
illusion, the self-deception that
"all *is* well" rather than
"all *shall be* well," the
dwelling place of Hope.

Optimism can seduce us
into failing to take reality-
what IS- seriously...

Hope is more rugged, more muscular...
building up its strength in the heavy
lifting of the way things *are*- and
carrying them- toward a better way
a new day.

Hope is the voice and promise of
endurance, of courage, of faith...
and it comes with a price,
requires work, with no assurance
of a rosy outcome.

Hope is what gets us through &
beyond when the worst that
can happen happens.
Hope grounds us
supports us
lifts us
Hope floats.

102.

April 21

It is inclusivity that brings security-
belonging, not belongings.
-Jeremy Rifkin

thin places

Thin places...
  where boundaries between
  light & darkness blur...
  where eternity rubs close
  to the world of time...
                    luminous...
                    numinous...
                    mysterious...
No words can explain...
  only the language
    of the heart- unspoken,
                    yet completely,
                        deeply real...
In the hands of God,
permitting ourselves to be
bearers of comfort & hope
  to a hurting person
  to a hurting world,
    WE are thin places-
    where the visible &
              invisible worlds
              rub against each other...
    where we stand
      on the threshold,
      taking what we have been
      given & living life-
        in all its incredible beauty-
                    luminous...
                    numinous...
                    mysterious.

April 22

This I know,
That the only way to live
is like the rose
which lives
without a why.
-Meister Eckhart

another morning prayer
Grant peace in my heart
   this day, O God.
Breathe into me the joy
   of living fully,
   of loving totally,
   of forgiving myself
         and others.
Strengthen me to walk
   the path of truth...
   to make each step of
     my journey one
     of integrity &
     honesty.
Grace me with the courage
   to be true to my beliefs...
        to my friends...
        to my principles...
        to my creative talents...
And bless me with the
   gift of laughter,
      LOUD & LONG & JOYFUL!!!
     my YES to life.
       Amen

April 23

The consciousness of divinity is divinity itself. -Annie Dillard

psalm for a new day
I hear bird voices...
   wren & robin, dove & mockingbird
   rehearsing for the
    day ahead...

preparing to welcome
the still-sleeping sun...
"Rise & rejoice,"
their chorus rings...
"A new day looms,
filled with choice...
filled with hours &
minutes to use
as your choose..."

Oh, God, through whose
wisdom the world
came to be...
O God, who created
the songbirds-
and me, sitting here
in my room,
contemplating the
day ahead...
I offer my thanks...
my heartfelt gratitude...
for another new day
for friends near & far
for family who challenge &
cherish
for a mind that can think &
a heart that can feel
for the many moments
being presented to me
on the silver platter of
morning...

May I be as true to my
self & my calling
as the cardinal who
has now joined
the avian choir...
and may I bring
as much beauty-
and pure joy.
O God, it is truly enough!

April 24

A broken crystal glass, shattered into pieces, yet reflecting & refracting the light shining through the dining room window...a reminder that brokenness does not mean the end of things, the end of life, just its reshaping, its reformation.

shattered

A life shattered...
   yet redemption
   can come from
     the broken shards-
       if we let it...
       if we pick up the pieces...
         see the beauty of each one
           and know-
        even as we put them
        back together,
         things will never
          be the same...
         brokenness will always
         be there...
    yet we will be re-shaped
         re-formed
          resurrected...
   with scars & gaps & cracks
   where the light
      can shine t h r o u g h...

April 25

In the end, faith is less a set of beliefs than your willingness
to surrender to a mysterious force of love and guidance
that helps you find your way.
-Joan Z. Borysenko

not knowing

We investigate-
   because we *don't know...*
We question-
   because we *don't know...*
We imagine-
   because we *don't know...*

And in the seeking,
        asking,
            imagining,
    we open ourselves to
        new possibilities!
Creativity blooms!
New life emerges!
After all,
    isn't certainty-
        rather than doubt-
            the opposite of faith?
If we KNOW,
    have no doubts,
        no questions,
    where is the need for
        the room for
            faith?

April 26

Being alert to, aware of, thankful for the everyday things of life is perhaps the greatest gift we can give ourselves- but all too seldom do.

an ordinary day

So begins the day-
    fragrant, hot coffee
    a distant train whistle
    a wavering bird call
    flickering candlelight
    gray outside-light
    a stack of whites awaiting laundering
    a second of darks strewn carelessly
    rumpled bed set aright
            and now to dress
            and stretch
            and walk
            and later to eat-
                and so enter fully
                another day.
                IT IS ENOUGH.

April 27

and it came to pass...

The Bible's "And it came to pass..."
Elie Wiesel's "And yet..."
the Tao's "Life IS life..."
words of wisdom & comfort, all...
    but we want things to be different
    than they are...want assurances...
    want the bases covered...
        only that is not Life!
Life is the unfolding of *moments*...
the tick of the clock...the strains of
Barber's "Adagio"...the fragrance of
fresh coffee...the distant sounds of
traffic...the warble of birds...the
hum of the furnace...the shadow of
my hand on the page...the growl
        of my empty stomach.
It is walking with deliberation &
joy...with awareness & gratitude,
eyes wide open, heart attuned to
the pace, the rhythm of your own
beating heart, to the pulse
        of the world's living energy...
It is caring deeply enough about
your today and other's tomorrows
that you make wise & heartfelt decisions
        about using, spending, wasting...
It is spending your *life* profligately,
unconcerned about saving it for
a rainy day but splashing through
the puddles in joyous awareness that
rain is as necessary for life as
sunshine...that light comes only
after darkness...that awe & wonder
are the only truly appropriate
responses to this incredible
        gift that is TODAY!

108.

April 28

*Make every word you speak count,
and you will co-create with God.*
-Alan Cohen

words

How I love words,
                language...
How I delight in the
    images words can
    create in my
            mind's eye...
    the pictures they
    can paint,
            inviting me in...
What else has such power?
Can this be what it means
    to be made in
        the image of God?

April 29

poetry

What makes writing poetry
    rather than prose?
Is it something in the
    pen of the writer...
    the eye of the reader?
Is it cadence or thought,
        image or idea?
I cannot define it-
    yet I know it when
    I read it- or hear it...
I am left untouched,
I must confess,
    by the deliberately pretentious-
    those purporting great
        depth of meaning
        buried beneath the
            words offered...

Mining for meaning
leaves me exhausted!
What I seek is simply
an "Ah" or "Aha" as
my soul is touched...
a smile on my lips or
a tear on my cheek...
Some phrases take my
breath away...
others awe in their
simplicity...
some fall deep into
my heart...
still others stab my
awareness with the
sword of truth...
and some fall as flat
as the proverbial
pancake...
So- who decides about greatness?
From whence comes value?
I wonder...

There is no hidden poet in me, just a little piece of God
that might grow into poetry.
-Etty Hillesum

April 30

An overcast day, with rain predicted for this afternoon. I guess it has affected
my mood, for what comes to mind is the abandoned robin's nest just off the
back deck...so, with a salute to Mary Oliver, here is my morning offering.

empty nest

An empty nest,
so carefully begun with
diligent labor and many
furtive trips
of he and she,
both working hard to craft
that cradle to receive
the sky-blue eggs...

Why did they choose this
spot, so near to all of my
  comings-and-goings?
The noisy ups-and-downs
  of leather shoes on
  wooden stairs...
the slowly-closing hesitation
  of the screen door...
What made the chosen place,
at first a haven of sorts amidst
the drooping branches, become
instead a place of threat?
    for now it stands abandoned...
    disintegrating slowly in the
    recent heavy winds...
reminder of what
might have been-
  but never will...
of dream's potential
  left undone
of heart's hope
  abandoned...
that intermingling
  of life & death which
  marks the journey of
          each day,
          each life.

reflections...

MAY-
the merry month

May 1

My dear sister, Susan, reminded me that today is 'May Day', recalling how, as children, we used to make little baskets, fill them with wild flowers- usually violets- and leave them on doorknobs in the neighborhood. Do children do that any more? And wouldn't it be lovely if they did? Wouldn't it be lovely if we all did?

May Day!

May Day! May Day!
Planes targeting buildings
  filled with ordinary
   people doing ordinary
        things...
suicide bombers targeting
  people they don't even
  know in order to
  lay claim to a heaven only reached
       by the hell they create...
a gun-wielding, mentally-ill
  young man, acting out
  of his pain and perverted
  world-view, shooting
  fellow-students, faculty,
       for reasons beyond reason...

May Day! May Day!
The world is going to hell
  in a bushel basket-
    fear runs rampant!
    life is out of control!
    the foundations shaken...
       no place to stand
       no place that is safe...

May Day! May Day!
Tiny baskets, flowers overflowing,
  hung on doorknobs,
  bringing a taste of spring...
  carrying the fragrance
       of hope...
Loving messages of care
  and concern sent

via the mysterious
electronic gift of e-mail...
carrying & conveying the
ongoing connection of
heart to heart,
life to life...
A phone call from a loving
child to say hello, to say
"I care"...to light the day
with long-distance love,
no less the sweet for being
conveyed from afar...

May Day! May Day!
A cry for help...
a cry of hope-
and love
and joy
and eternal connection-
and life!
I choose LIFE-
and it is enough!

May 2

We judge and punish based on facts, but facts are not truth.
Facts are like a buried skeleton uncovered long after death.
Truth is fluid. Truth is alive. To know the truth requires
understanding, the most difficult human art. It requires seeing
all things at once, forward and backward, the way God sees.
-Greg Iles

questions without answers

Differences without divisiveness-
shouldn't that be possible?
Shouldn't it be possible to
agree to disagree?
Why should it be a necessity
that one opinion or set of beliefs
wins out over another?

And yet, there ARE issues which matter...
issues of peace & justice & respect for

human dignity & the care of this earth...
      and how do we back off from those?
How do I honor the beliefs
of someone whose position on matters
   which go to the core of
   my beliefs is diametrically   opposite mine?
How do I refrain from taking
   a stand which to some might seem
   naive or foolish, even heretical,
   when my heartfelt beliefs call
   me to do so?

What is the price of silence?
           of debate?
   And whose "truth" is true?
                I don't know...
                I'm just asking...

May 3

to-do list

How do I approach this day?
   with tentative steps-
      or **bold strides?**
There is much to be done...
a long list of to-dos...
   both ordinary and significant...
   routine and off-the-wall...
Grant me focus,
  O Creative Spirit...
   inbreathe me with
     purpose & diligence...
   and sweeten it with
    joy & gratitude.
         Let it be so.

May 4
Can I leave it all behind? the myriad demands which life places on me, which I place on myself? Can I grant myself the gift & grace of one day of holiness outside the bounds of convention? And if not, WHY NOT?

today 2
To go at my own pace...
   a day without
      demands...
   no schedule to
      keep...
   no place to
      be...
   leaving behind
      "musts"
      "shoulds"
      "need-tos"
   and savoring
       relishing
       celebrating
         the wonder
         of the being I am.
This is a gift
  I can give to myself...
  and today,
     I receive it with o   p   e   n   arms.

May 5
Our consciousness is not continuous,
but a sequence of 'ah-ha moments'.
-Stuart Hameroff

order
I have learned a truth-
at least for me:
   order in my outer world leads to,
   creates order in my inner world.
Of course, this can be taken
to extremes, like any truth...
   obsession & compulsion
   belie the gift of inner peace.

But when my desk & study,
bedroom, closets, & refrigerator
are orderly & neat, freed of
clutter & detritus, the
flotsam & jetsam of life I
so often accumulate,
   my breathing slows...
   creative energy flows...
   the blessing of simplicity &
   simply living...
   both the "Ah!" and "Aha"
      of opening up my mind.

May 6

*Thoughts are energy. And you can make your world or
break your world by your thinking.* -Susan L. Taylor

self-talk

Not to claim & risk
your possibilities is to
   abandon your SELF...
Walk into the unknown...
   dare to fail...dare to succeed...
   dare to live by
         what you value...
Live faithfully...
   even when you're
   not sure what
      faith means...
See the glass as half-full....
Know that sharing the water is
   what life is all about...
Choose to walk
   instead of crawl-
         or just sit there...
Value & celebrate
   what's left...
This is what today
   is all about- and today is
         what you have...and IT IS ENOUGH.
118.

May 7

*The world cannot be discovered by a journey of miles, no matter how long,
but only by a spiritual journey, a journey of one inch, very arduous and
humbling and joyful, by which we arrive at the ground at our feet
and learn to be at home.* **-Wendell Berry**

time-less

I have the sense of
time slipping through
my fingers.
   I long to grab hold,
   cling tightly, make
   today last & last & last...
      so much to be done
      so much to be said
      so much I long to accomplish

But time, like a river,
flows steadily on...and therein
lies its beauty...moment to
moment never the same...each
drop, each breath, each second
different from the one before...
the strange & mysterious
effluence of life.

   So- can I go with the flow,
   instead of swimming upstream?
   Can I make time my friend...
         embrace it...
         open to it...
         let it move in & through &
         around me?
   Can I let go of the frantic
   desire to grasp & control it,
   and instead accept, value, &
   use it as the gift it is...
         the present...
         the now.

May 8

As I have mentioned, outside of my bedroom window stands the most beautiful Japanese maple tree. When I sit in my small rattan chair, I feel as if I am part of her; her changes mark my seasons, and she is home to the birds as she is surely home to me, as I sit in my 'tree house' to read & think & write.

nesting

I didn't see them building it,
the nest now nestled in the
tree outside my window,
almost near enough to touch.
But there it is, sturdy
and safe even in the
buffeting winds which toss
the treetops to and fro and
scatter papers from my desk
when I fling windows open wide
to welcome the outdoors inside.
When I peer out, several times
each day, she sits in regal
majesty, the robin, perhaps
on sky-blue eggs, precursors
of the baby birds whose chirps
will fill my room with welcome
noise before too long...
    life going on...the cycle never-ending...
        new & fresh & holy.
            I take a breath- and offer thanks.

May 9

We are light through a prism. The light is always there, but only we can act as its prism, concentrate and filter it. We make of the light of the cosmos, a rainbow with a mouth and arms. -Jarrett Smith

light

The sun is up...
and so the day begins...
    my heart wrapped around
    the Truth of God's Presence-
        in me...in the world...here & now.

I inbreathe this reality...
I inbreathe the Presence...
   I am filled.
The light of God shines
   through the broken
      places...the cracks
         in my life...
            not as a beacon
            but as a flickering
                     ember.
May it light the way
   for someone else today.
               IT IS ENOUGH.

May 10

The spirituality of the American Indian peoples is deeply connected with the earth, the earth deeply connected with the people, and the people with one another. Their honor of the holiness and wholeness of creation carries a beauty & wonder which I love and which resonates deeply with my own soul.

prayer of the Ojibway people

Grandfather,
Look at our brokenness.

We know that in all creation
Only the human family
Has strayed from the Sacred Way.

We know that we are the ones
Who are divided
And we are the ones
Who must come back together
To walk the Sacred Way.

Grandfather,
Sacred One,
Teach us love, compassion, and honour
That we may heal the earth
and heal each other.

May 11

You be perfectly you, let me be perfectly me: uniquely and mutually flawed.
And together we can discover what it is to be human,
and what two humans might be capable of being together.
-Joy Houghton

story telling

If you tell me your story,
and I tell you mine,
   a bridge of trust is
   built between us over
   which our hearts & souls
   can traverse freely, in delight & gratitude.

If you tell me your story,
and I tell you mine,
   releasing both hate & harm,
   we feel understood...
         acccepted...
         seen...

If you tell me your story,
and I tell you mine,
   together we drink deeply
   of the refreshing water of life,
   the source of what is true & good,
   our thirst for intimacy satisfied
         if only for this moment.

If you tell me your story,
and I tell you mine,
   we stand with arms wide open
   to receive the offering of
   fears & failings, joys & triumphs,
   holding & upholding one another
   in mutual respect & shared support.

So- you tell me your story,
and I will tell you mine-
   and we can transform
   life's journey *together.*

122.

May 12

What frightens us might also have the power to transform us.
-Barbara Hurd

fear

When I am afraid of doing something...
when I hesitate, procrastinate, avoid...
remind me, Spirit of Daring & Truth,
that the very thing which
      taunts & pulls
      pushes & challenges
        is in my life to *do*
          those things...
        to break down my finely-
          honed defenses,
        to pull down my well-
          built walls of protection,
        to make me face the truth!
For when I do, to my amazement and
delight, I find I am able to do the very thing
I had believed I could not do.
        Hallelujah! and amen.

May 13

To change one's life, start immediately, do it flamboyently,
with no exceptions. -William James

Spirit speaks

Let your heart burn with love.
Truth exists...live in it.
Speak only from the heart.
I encircle you...
  guard you...
  guide you...
Take my hand...
take the risk.
There is nothing to fear.
    Trust your heart...hear its truth.
    Take small steps- but be willing
        to run through the treetops!

Let dreams accompany you.
This IS your life...expend it wisely...
wander in the wilderness...
face the wildness...
Carry me with you
every living moment.
Open your heart to inner direction...
I am the truth...
nothing separates us...
let your spirit soar!
There are no limits.
BELIEVE THAT.
Let it carry you.
Create knowingly, lovingly, truthfully.
It is enough.

May 14

morning plea

Grant me peace today, O Wise One,
Mother God.

Grant me rest today,
as I seek to let go of problems
beyond my ability to solve.

Grant me joy today-
some small measure of love &
tenderness which touches
my heart's pain.

Grant me laughter today-
rumbling from deep within,
releasing what has been
held captive there.

And if tears should come, gather me
in your arms & hold me close, this
wounded, hurting child of yours.
amen & amen
124.

May 15

*Genuine forgiveness is participation, reunion overcoming
the power of estrangement...We cannot love unless
we have accepted forgiveness, and the deeper our experience
of forgiveness, the greater our love.* -**Paul Tillich**

the gift

When I am dealing with
a deep issue, a heartfelt
problem, I do not want
the advice of someone,
                anyone, else.

I do not want
to be fixed or saved.
   What I *do* want is
   a listening ear,
   an open heart,
   a mirror held up in front of me
      so I can see myself as
      I am and as I might
      become...
   an open space in which
      transformation can happen,
      as the answer arises from
      deep within myself.
I need the intimacy of
presence...the healing of
acceptance...the wonder of
compassion, so that I can
speak my own inner truth.
         So, if I know this
         about myself,
         why am I so slow in
         offering that gift to you?

May 16

Having my ninety-one year old mother living with me makes me ever aware of the process of aging...provides me with a kind of 'practice' for the years ahead...makes me wonder what it will be like to be old...rather than simply 'aging'.

aging

What is it like
to be just past ninety-one,
in good overall health
   with a clear mind-
only to have your
skeleton begin to
   fall apart?
Is there a sense of
betrayal- as the body
cared for so diligently
       so faithfully
  STILL begins to deteriorate
         to let you down?

And which is worse,
I wonder from my
"only" sixty-six years-
   to have a declining body
   and an aware mind-
      OR
   to have a declining mind
   which no longer knows or cares
   in a healthy body?

No answers here...
   only questions...
   upon questions
   upon questions...

126.

May 17

*There will always be enough uncertainty to make life sizzle
and renew our sense of wonder.* **-Diane Ackerman**

life lessons
Have you ever said this:
"I did it *again...*
when am I going to learn?"
ALWAYS...NEVER...
So...invite in those parts of
yourself you would rather not
admit...befriend and learn from
them...don't hurry to send them
away or, even worse, deny their
presence. You cannot swallow
life whole...rather, take bite
after bite...chew thoroughly...
then let it digest...and you
will be fed & nourished.
Life is about embracing
paradox...
   by unlearning you learn
   by slowing down you can soar
   by not insisting that things make sense
     you gain insight
   by not "growing up" you grow
   by letting go you become who
     you were meant to be.

May 18

*Even if you're on the right track, you'll get run over if
you just sit there.* **-Will Rogers**

choice
Have you ever considered
that overcommitment
is the sign of a lack-
     of self-value, self-worth,
       self-esteem?
Refusing to set boundaries,
to guard carefully your own time,

your own sense of yourself,
  is giving in to someone else's
  definition of who you are...
  is giving up the essence
  of who you *really are.*
The only person who can rightfully
"name" you is YOU...from the
  inside out.
The only person who can rightfully
claim your time & energy is YOU...
  and you share yourself by CHOICE.
Today is a new day...
a day of your life you
are trading away- for what?
    May the choice be yours-
    and may it give you joy!

May 19

May mating

The air is alive with birds!
I can't recall ever seeing
so many at one time before...
  The mating time, I guess...
  with all its flutterings & sounds...
  as tentatively yet noisily,
  pairs are formed...
and elsewhere in the yard, chicks
are chirpingly encouraged to take
flight by pairs whose earlier
mating led to nest-held eggs,
long days of brooding, more days
of faithful feeding-
  and that last nudge
  as reluctant offspring
  leave the nesting safety
  and tentatively fly
    into the waiting world.

May 20

These words were written for my daughter, Hope, whose mothering skills and devotion to my granddaughter, Lindsay, leave me awestruck. And though I have told her so many times, I don't think I could ever tell her often enough.

Mothers' Day

I look into her lovely face
and catch tiny glimpses of
my own, far deeper imprints
of her dad...yet she is surely,
fully, and completely
her own person...
   convictions deep & wide
   and lived out...
      her body shaped by
      healthy food, by bike-riding
      and yoga...
      her spirit formed by care
      for the environment, the
      earth & all its creatures...
      her heart broken open again &
      yet again by love & rejection,
                hope & disappointment,
                acquisition & loss-
      yet most of all,
         by mothering...
         by giving life to her
           own daughter,
         by loving her into being
           her own loving, giving,
                beautiful self...
      and in so doing,
         giving us both the
         most incredible gift
           of all...
               the lovely young woman
               that is my granddaughter,
                 Lindsay.

May 21

It is extraordinary what a difference there is between understanding a thing and knowing it by experience. **Teresa of Avila**

heaven

What is "heaven"-
and where?
Is the "reward" of
God's grace & presence
not *here*- in the present?
in the enrichment & fullness
of our lives as we follow
in the path of the One
who taught & lived compassion?
Can we not leave the
"heaven" language
behind- perhaps instead
use "eternity" if we need
a word, though who know
what *that* actually means!
Does seem more whole,
somehow...more honest...
especially since
we really have no
idea of the where &
when &
how of either word.
Perhaps...and
I am only thinking
out loud here...
perhaps what we should
really focus upon is love
hope
justice
compassion
HERE & NOW...
leaving "heaven" & "eternity"
firmly in the "hands"
of Divine Wisdom.

130.

May 22

For me, writing is about telling the truth; taking the risk of making myself vulnerable, transparent. And I have found that when I share my darkest places, my deepest feelings, there is always someone who says, 'Yes! That is exactly how I feel!', verifying my leap of faith.

care-taking

I am so tired of
being responsible...
    shopping & cooking &
        pulling weeds...
    paying bills & doing laundry
        & keeping things in order...
I am so tired of
taking care of!
    Why can't someone
    take care of *me*
        for a change?
There- I said it...
words coming from deep inside,
    an empty, longing place...
    a void...
    a crater...
which only a relationship
    could fill...a "partner" in the
        deepest, truest sense...
    someone with whom
        to travel...to share joys & sorrows...
    someone who could
        share my *life*...
I guess I just miss
being hugged & kissed &
    held & touched...

And God, with my apologies to you,
sometimes I need
    God with *skin on*...
And friends, with my apologies to you,
sometimes, it seems,
    friendship is *not*
        enough...

(perhaps I really need
    a dog rather than
    a man...I don't know...)

What I do know is
I sound like a petulant
    child-
        but this is how I feel
        today.
            Tomorrow- who knows?

*What lies behind us and what lies before us are tiny matters
compared to what lies within us.*
-Oliver Wendell Holmes

May 23

meditation...

Sit still.

Inspire...breathe...fill yourself with
                God's own Ruach.

Let go- of schedules, cares,
                shoulds & musts.

Enter the holy place within where Spirit dwells,
                where self is true...

Numinous, mysterious,
                the threshold, the thin place
                between human & divine.

Contemplate...consent to...celebrate the holiness
                of your life.

Expire...breathe out all that has kept you
                bound & dwell- even for a
                moment-
                        in EXALTATION!

132.

May 24

*To live wholly or holy is not to reach for some otherness
but to penetrate deeply into each moment, hour, or season.*
-Joan Anderson

healing

Healing, I believe,
is loving & accepting yourself
as you are-
        here & now.
When we seek for
perfection, some
imagined ideal person
we are *supposed* to be-
or so we think- we lose
sight of the incredible,
amazing fact of our
unique reality- today-
        at this time & place.
Every moment up till now,
every happening & choice,
every word & every deed,
every person, every place,
every book & every song,
every laugh & every tear,
every truth & every lie,
every hope & every dream,
every failure or success-
        EVERYTHING-
            has made us who we are...
So welcome that dear person.
Embrace her or him
    with loving warmth.
Smile at all you have become-
    and you will be
            healed.

May 25

Bless to me, O Creator God, this new day.

Bless my eyes to see the
  new opportunities...to see
  the familiar in a new way.

Bless my ears to hear
  not only the sounds of the
  voices of others but of my
  own voice...making of
  my words a blessing.

Bless my actions this day
  and remind me of the possibility
  woven deep within each moment...
  as I stand at the brink of choice
  again & again & yet again.

Bless my heart to feel both
  the joy & pain of living,
  to celebrate the reality of
  both unity & separateness...
  the gift of darkness & light...
  the holiness of the ordinary
  and the ordinary presence of the holy.

Bless for me this day, O God,
  and for all I love...
  and all who need my love.
  Let me enter the world of gentle possibility
    with each breath I take...and may I breathe
    a blessing with every word
                              deed
                              thought
                              hope...
                    Let it be so. Amen

May 26

My favorite writing place these days is called 'Healing Ground', the home/ retreat center of two dear friends who make the studio space available to me for several hours each week. Being at a remove from my familiar home and all that calls to me there...the peace, the beauty, the silence... all are stimuli to creativity...and so I write.

music

I listened to several of
Bach's "Brandenburg
Concertos" this morning
and was transported...
dozed off last night to the
sublime blend of voices in
"Les Miserables"...danced
in the afternoon to the
irresistible rhythms of "Smoky
Joe's Café"...then sat outdoors
moments ago hearing the
whisper of the wind in the
trees, the murmur of the
fountain on the hill, the
call of the birds overhead...
   immersed in
   surrounded by
      music of every sort...
aware that the
melodies & harmonies
create a wholeness...
bringing my inner & outer
worlds into
     harmonious oneness...
    written with beauty
    on the staff of my life...
    a song sung in many
    keys but always in
      my own voice.

Writers perfect
The art
Of doing nothing
So beautifully.
    -Alice Walker

135.

May 27

no rain

An over-cast morning...
   will today perhaps
   bring rain to
   this small corner
   of the world?
All around, storms
   have been crashing...
      while the arms of
      my flowers reach
         skyward,
         beseeching...
      and then droop languidly
      in despair
         as their prayers go
            unanswered.

May 28

grateful green

The birds are singing
noisily early this morning...
and the ground is
heaving great sighs
of joy & gratitude
for the recent rains.
No watering needed
today...my herbs &
flowers thrive...the
earth is watered
and green and
verdant.
   Praise &
   thanksgiving!

136.

May 29

...we are invited to forget ourselves on purpose, cast our awful solemnity to the winds and join in the general dance. -**Thomas Merton**

sometimes...

Sometimes I think too much
and my spirit tires with the effort...
   I want to disengage my brain
   and simply BE-
              feel
              absorb
              revel in the
        sights & sounds & smells
        around me
  without thinking it through...
without weighing or
        analyzing or
          trying to figure it out or
            make connections
To savor the flavor of early morning
   coffee on my tongue
To inhale the fragrance
of that same coffee-
   and the earthy aroma
   of the garden beneath
   my open window
To get lost in the sound
of the songbirds saluting
   the new day
To await with eager anticipation
the rising of the sun through my
   east-facing bedroom windows
         and NOT to question
            to figure any of it out
        only to enjoy &
          absorb &
          sink into the
          realities of this
            new day.
              AH!

May 30

This work to be done called for this life.
-Maurice Merleau-Ponty

memorial day

We remember-
those who fought and died
   to give this nation birth,
   in the face of unremitting odds...

those who fought and died
   to keep this nation unified,
   in spite of our differences...

those who fought and died
   on foreign soil to restore peace
   and freedom to the places of
   our long-ago roots, to the *world*...

those who fought and died
   in a police action which
   never really ended...

those who fought and died
   in a tiny southeast Asian
   country while a war of words &
   ideologies raged on home shores...

those who fought and died
   in the deserts of the Gulf
   for reasons which remain
   unclear & unclarified...

those who continue to fight and die
   in Iraq and Afghanistan because
   our nation is afraid to face
   its own shortcomings & failings...

We remember-
   or are we choosing to forget?

138.

May 31

another TODAY...

I cannot live tomorrow
        today...
to worry about it
        is fruitless...
        it destroys peace of mind.
I CAN HANDLE RIGHT NOW...
  so- plan, not worry...
      planning empowers,
      worry victimizes.
I have the courage
    the inner resources
      to handle whatever
      happens today.

reflections...

JUNE -
the green season

June 1

When you're traveling the terrain of time, the shortest distance between two points may be a detour. -**Marjorie Kelly**

roadblocks
Sometimes roadblocks mean
   you are being directed to
         diverted to
    a special road...
       one that will take
         all of your focus...
         all of your energy...
         all of your courage
           to overcome
           the obstacles.
Be aware...
be open to learn
    when it is time
    to search for
        another road...
      OR
    when it is time
    to move forward
       through
       the obstacles
         to achieve your dream.

June 2

The day of my spiritual awakening was the day I saw- and knew I saw- all things in God and God in all things.
-**Mechtilde of Magdeburg**

regard the birds...
Curious, isn't it, how
completely the birds abandon
their nests after the
nestlings have flown?
Where do they live the
remainder of the time?
It's not like the trees
are filled with birds

on perches, even in foul
weather...so where do
they go at night? during
storms? when our human
tendency is to seek shelter,
to go home. I hear them now,
these feathered denizens
of nature, awake long
before the first signs
of dawn, their songs
harbingers of a lovely
day to come. Or are they
simply being birds,
living out their God-given
purpose, living from their
core with such apparent
ease? 'They toil not, neither
do they spin', yet what
would our world be like
without them?

June 3

*What is the difference between a psalm & a prayer? For me, it is the
attitude...the tone...the awareness of gratitude...the awareness of being
in the Presence of what I call God. Does that make sense? I don't know...
some writings are just 'psalms'...they name themselves.*

another psalm for a new day

I open my heart, Loving, Living God.
I place myself in your hands...
I breathe in the beauty of the rising sun...
I savor the gift of another day
                              of life...
Wherever this day leads,
    let me rest in the assurance
    of your presence with me, in me,
                    under & around me...
Let me taste every moment
    and savor it all.
Hold me in your loving arms and breathe
    into me the blessing of peace...

Remove from my heart all fear, all anxiety
                    all that keeps me bound
                    and threatens my freedom
                                my growth...
For in you I find refuge...
    in you I find welcome...
    in you I find justice & hope...
    in you I find my fullest self.
                And it is ENOUGH.

June 4

The function of prayer is not to influence God, but rather to change the nature of the one who prays. -**Soren Kierkegaard**

stuck- a psalm

Unstick me, O God.
Pull me from this
    mire of self-pity and anxiety
    in which I have
            caught myself.
Remove from me
    all fear- about the future
                about my finances
                about my health
                about my children & grandchildren.
Help me to accept & embrace
    all of life,
        no matter what it brings,
    confident that the strength
    to see it through WILL
    be there, as it has always been
                in the past.
You are my rock, my firm ground...
    under your wings I hide...
    in your arms I find comfort...
    from you I draw my strength
                my hope
                my courage.
Help me to live this day
                wisely & well. Amen & amen
144.

June 5

another conundrum...
CLEAVE...to cut apart...
     a meat cleaver, rending the meat,
        what was once living, breathing flesh...
     cutting it into culinarily-acceptable
        pieces...making it seem okay to
        be ingesting parts of another
        living creature.
CLEAVE...
    so how can it also mean
        "to cling"? to be joined to?
What a contradiction in terms!
    Marrying couples promise to cleave...
       to cling to one another...
       to unite hearts & lives...
    but what happens when a
       cleaver does the cleaving?
    when infidelity or indifference
      or anything else-
          sometimes just the grinding
          away by the daily grind-
      splits the relationship
            w   i   d   e   open,
           rends hearts & lives?
              What then?
Flesh cut apart cannot again
    be joined...
       lamb chops & rack of lamb &
       roast lamb can never again
       be the white, wooly creatures
         calmly grazing in
            the pasture...
So, can a relationship which
    has been cleaved apart ever again
    be one in which the two cleave
        and become one flesh?
Can it ever truly be?
    I don't know...
       I wonder...I wonder deeply.   145.

June 6

truth-telling

Telling the truth
takes courage...
often enormous courage-
     and strength...
        to face my fears...
           my self-doubts...
           my need to conform...
           my need for approval...

How much easier to follow the crowd...
        to kowtow to authority...
        to accede to popular opinion...
than to stand on my own two legs,
admittedly with knees knocking,
and hold my ground.

And yet, I know I must
be true to what I *know*...
    to what life has taught me...
    to the voice of the Christ calling me
        from scripture's page, echoing in
        my heart, in my life...singing words
        of justice, peace, inclusion, compassion,
        hope, and love, the lilting melody
        discordant with the prevailing dirge
        of nation, church, & world,
    while the winds of the Spirit lift
    the tune of genuine, holy love
    and carry it to the farthest
    reaches of space...
    and to the depths of each
    receptive human heart.

June 7

*The real voyage of discovery lies not in discovering new lands,
but in seeing with new eyes.* -Marcel Proust

can you imagine?

Can you imagine yourself
   as one manifestation
      of the consciousness
      of the universe?
   as a momentary explosion
      of God-energy?
   as an in-this-moment
   embodiment
      of the spiritual energy
         of the universe?
      of the Force of
         Healing & Transformation?
Allow yourself to experience-
         to feel-
         to comprehend-
   how incredible
    it is to be alive!
You are- at this very
   moment- the latest unfolding
      of the event of Creation...
created in the image of God
    to reflect the outpouring of
    Divine love & generosity.
         Can you imagine?

June 8

*Whenever we wait to do something that will make a difference, whether
we realize it or not, we are making a difference by doing nothing at all.*
-Joan Chittister

prayer for connection

Live deep within me,
   Holy Oneness.
Fill me with the awareness
   of the holiness of all of life,
   that I may live from

that truth...
the truth that we are all
part of you...
part of one another...
Breathe into me the breath of life
this day, that I may
live fully, with integrity,
and with a deepening
sense of community &
connectedness...
I do not understand the
systems of this world which
keep us bound...
am not usually aware of
my own complicity in them-
yet ignorance is no
excuse- for inaction or
for apathy...
Free me from the cowardice
of doing nothing...
from the self-righteousness
of thinking the little I do is
sufficient.
Connect me to the community
of humanity- in my heart
and in my life.
Let it be so.

June 9

Sometimes the world closes in and nature seems to mirror the state of my life, my concerns amassing like clouds on the horizon, and finally breaking like a storm over which I have no control.

passing storm

Outside, the wind
is moaning...
I hear the wind chimes
ringing their mournful lament.
Rain comes in gusts &
the sky is battleship gray.
School buses continue to run,

their startling yellow transporting
children, telling me that life is
going on as usual.
But how has the coast fared,
I wonder.
How are my daughter
and her kitten doing?
What will my granddaughter's
scan show?
Oh God, oh God, oh God-
no other words come-
only this plaintive cry-
and here I dwell,
my emotions mirroring
the stormy grayness
outside as the very
world seems
locked in
lamentation.

reflections...

June 10

In spite of the natural beauty of June, in spite of a world of green and light all around me, I found myself looking at life through gray-clouded glasses... though I am unsure why. Perhaps it was just part of the on-going cycle of life: a reminder that with the good comes the bad, with joy comes sadness, with life comes death. We are human, after all...with all that entails. And so, for a number of days, my writing reflected the place of refuge & reflection to which my heart retreated.

living & dying...

Bless the moments, O God...
    the breaths I take,
    the steps I make,
    the love I give & receive...
    the wondrous hope of
        life existing- and
    the incredible sorrow of
        life ending...
        a two-year-old dying...
        a soldier being blown apart...
        an elderly woman slipping away...
        a teen killed by a drunk driver....
   yet all of it part of that endless cycle
   which I do not begin to understand.
Life hangs heavy...
  can I grasp the
    joy again? God willing...

*Although the world is very full of suffering,
it is also full of the overcoming of it.*
-Helen Keller

June 11

morning greeting

The day is beginning fully. My tree
holds an early-morning robin as
comfortably as my little wicker
chair holds me. The sun has yet
to make an appearance, though
the sky has been lightening for

nearly two hours. I love the hushed
voice of the ceiling fan, offering its
one-note accompaniment to the
melodic symphony of morning birds.
Oh! A ray of sunlight has penetrated
the trees...a jogger heads down the
street toward Sunset...a white minivan
goes in the opposite direction...a few
more swallows of coffee remain in the
red mug- then I head into the yard-
to plant, pull, lug, water- to tend this
plot of earth on which I am planted,
rejoicing in being here,
           being alive,
           being humanly aware,
           just BEING.

June 12
Debate, doubt, and questioning are the signs of a lively faith. **-John L. Bell**

adrift
O God of my heart,
   from where does this
   bereftness come?
      this longing?
      this aching loneliness?
Everyone, it seems, has
purpose, focus, calling,
    except me...
And I feel adrift...
cast out into a stormy sea
  with no shore in sight
  and my small boat no match
  for the pounding waves...
Gray sky...grayer sea...
  and an enshrouding mist
  covers & encompasses me,
  sapping my strength,
       my will to go on.
Where are you in all this,
  O Divine One?

For if I believe anything at all,
it is that your presence
permeates all of life...
    even this cold gray mist...
        this barren, lonely sea...
        this dark night of my soul.
And in spite of my seeming
    aloneness,
        I am companioned
        by your Holy Oneness...
the emptiness of my boat
    an illusion,
        for you share with
        me the task of guiding
        it to the yet-unseen,
        far distant shore.
            Ah- the whispering sound
            of wings- and a sprig of green
            drops at my feet.
                land is in reach-
                and Hope springs once again.

June 13

adrift...again

Adrift on the ocean of life-
but not rudderless...
I trim my sails to catch the wind
    of the Spirit...
        holy Breath driving me to
            the unknown future-
eager anticipation fills my heart
        in spite of the uncertainty
        of where I will land...
I am accompanied...companioned...
        breathed into...guided by the One who Loves...
Here I am now...and for today...
    for this moment in time, IT IS ENOUGH.

152.

June 14

Early morning silence often yields an inner 'voice'... a sense of guidance. As I sit with pen in hand, words emerge, to which I have learned to pay serious attention. The voice of God? For me, yes.

inner voice

Guide me today,
    Precious Teacher, Inner Guide,
    Healing Spirit. Heal my fears...
And the voice speaks:
    Enter the deepest space,
       the place of openness.
    Dwell there.
    Come into this place of truth.
    Trust the person you are.
    Be true to your heart.
    The path is clear.
    Enlighten your way with words...
       listen carefully.
    Hope lies deep within-
       cling tightly but open your heart.
    Here & now is all you have
       and it is real.
    Let the dance of life carry you,
       the truth of life enfold you.
    Take a step back-
       the way becomes clear.
    Open your heart- lay it bare.
    Only then will healing happen.
    The path darkens but the way
       will unfold.
    Trust & believe...I am with you.
    Breathe in holiness...let go of striving...
       rest in this day...
       there is nothing to prove.
    You are perfect just as you are.
    Accept that I accept you.
    There is nothing to fear.
    I am with you.
    I am in you.
       It is enough.

June 15

I AM...
O Source of Life, Fountain of Strength,
Light of Hope & Forgiveness,
    soothe me with your healing balm,
    that my many self-inflicted wounds
    may finally heal...the heart broken by
    my failure to make good & wise decisions...
    the life misshapen by needs I did not
    begin to understand...the mind clouded by
    desires which narrow my vision...
    the body broken by dis-ease and misuse
    and neglect and disrespect...
So, now, I affirm that
I AM created in the
Divine Image...
    a dwelling place for
      the Holy...
    connected to all other
      life...
    beautiful & growing &
    alive with energy &
    hope...
    uniquely & amazingly myself...
I let go of anything which keeps me bound...
        which negates my growth...
        which tells me I am less than...
I hold this day
    this life in my hands...
      shared, as it is, with
      the community of humanity...
      the community of nature...
I breathe...I see...
I hear...I experience...
I feel...I choose...
I act...
I AM!!

*And did you get what
you wanted from this life, even so?
I did.
And what did you want?
To call myself beloved, to feel myself
beloved on the earth.*
      -Raymond Carver

June 16

Early morning...each day the sky lightens at an earlier hour. Time to reflect and write...to light the votive candle on my table, place my prayer shawl around my neck, pick up my pen, and open myself to the flow of creativity.

writing invocation

Come, Creative Spirit! Come, Light of Lights!
Breathe into me...enlighten me...
   break open my heart
      that my light may shine forth...
      that my voice may sing truth.
Forgive me, Creator God,
   for not trusting in the gifts
   you have given me...
   for allowing them to remain
   in the darkness instead of
   using them to your glory.
Shine the light of truth & hope
   upon them now and empower
   and embolden me to see
   myself as created co-creator...
   an artist with my own talent
         my own voice
         my own story to tell.
Surround and fill and enlighten
   me so that your creative energy
   flows through me.
       I believe; help my unbelief.

Writing is an act of cherishing...it is an act of love. -Julia **Cameron**

June 17

rebellion

What in the world
does it mean to be
    "well-adjusted"?
Adjusted well to what?
To the rules & expectations
    of our society? of our family?
    of our school? of our church?

Just who makes those "rules"-
   and why are *they* the ones
   making them?
Being "well-adjusted"
often means abdicating our uniqueness...
        betraying our true potential...
        denying our creativity & calling...
        turning away from the beat of
           a different drummer...
It means conformity
      for the sake of acceptance...
   living as less-than
      for the sake of approval...
   walking the well-trod path
      for the sake of inclusion...
   toeing the line
      for the sake of fitting in...
when all the while your heart is crying out,
   "It's your life!
     So why not dance?"

Life is either a daring adventure or nothing at all. -Helen Keller

June 18

new day dawning
In the first light of a new day,
I rest in your
   loving arms, Brother Christ.
I open myself to your
   ever-presence, Sister Spirit.
Open me to your reality in my life...
      to your indwelling of every living thing...
Bless me with congruity-
   outside & inside matching...
Let me be a woman of integrity,
    today & every day.

156.

June 19

God is many faces to many people- but all the same God.
-Joan Chittister

naming

I cannot name you, God...
  cannot explain you...
  cannot comprehend you...
I cannot define you...
  cannot grasp you...
So how can I believe?
      I do not know.
      I only say with the
          man who came to Jesus-
          "I believe- help my unbelief"-
And perhaps- it is enough.

June 20

i do not know

O God of Mystery,
    you & I have been at this thing
    called life for sixty-six years-
        and still I struggle- to understand
                            to comprehend
                            to know & be known.
I do not know who or how you are...
        and yet I know you with
        some deep
                intuitive sense...
        some mystical
                apprehension...
Life was simpler
    when my faith was
            simpler...
    but simplicity is difficult
    in a complex world-
        and mystery leads
        down a complex path...
            to where, I do not know.   157.

June 21

The Summer Solstice...the longest day of the year...summer truly & fully begun. A time to celebrate...a time to contemplate...a time to raise awareness...a time to care about the world in which we find ourselves.

uneasy green

Summer- lush & verdant...
weed growth run rampant...
a crazy-quilt of
    different shades of
      green...
Who knew green could be
  so many different colors?
    have so many varying
      personalities?

"It's not easy being green,"
was Kermit's long-ago lament...
  yet the foliage spreading
  far & wide seems
  not to share that sentiment,
    bursting forth in the
    riotous growth of vine &
      weed & flower & grass...
a green world,
    punctuated here & there
    by red & gold & purple-
      every rainbow shade-
        yet so much more...

What joy, what richness
to walk amidst this sensual feast,
    the world coming to life
    at the dawn of a new day-
      while across the world,
      bombs blast & the taste of cordite
        accompanies the evening meal.
        Lord, have mercy.

Life is ours to be spent, not to be saved. **-D.H. Lawrence**

158.

June 22

be my vision

Blessings today on all I love...
          on all the world...
          on the leaders of nations...
Let peace begin in
my heart this day...
open me to possibility...
          to joy...
          to the healing of my energy...
          to the healing of relationships...
Be my vision, O God...
     my guide
     my support
     my source of energy & strength.
                    LET IT BE SO.

June 23

continuing quest...

God of All Seeking & All Seekers,
     as my quest continues,
          let me be ever mindful
               of the present...
free me from jargon or
          easy answers...
dare me to plumb the depths
          and soar to the
               highest peak...
          to live fully &
               deeply &
               loftily & truly.
               IT IS ENOUGH.

*A very powerful question may not have an answer at the moment it is
asked. It will sit rattling in the mind for days or weeks as the person
works on an answer. If the seed is planted, the answer will grow.
Questions are alive.*
–Fran Peavey

159.

June 24

Remembering my dreams seems to run in cycles...and I will go for months, it seems, without recalling one image, without gleaning one insight. But on this particular morning, I awoke with the dream clearly in my mind and heart. And I was filled with joy!

dreaming

I dreamed that
I was singing love songs-
   to the world...
      joyously serenading
      this planet upon
      which we reside...
            you & I...
head thrown back
heart overflowing into
   irrepressible song...
      the rainbow-hued notes
      filling the air
      with beauty &
         laughter &
         joy
     VISIBLE...
     AUDIBLE...
     TANGIBLE!
And when I awoke, with
a smile on my face,
   I carried with me
   a sense of wholeness,
         completion-
as if my task
   had been accomplished...
      singing love songs
      to a hurting world.
         How lovely.
         How odd...

Dreams are necessary to life. -Anais Nin

June 25

*During my 'morning time' when I read & think & write, I wear a lovely,
handmade, multi-shaded blue prayer shawl around my neck, part of my
ritual to draw me into an awareness of Presence...of peace.*

on the fringe

Have I *ever* believed that
God causes everything
that happens? I don't think so.
It doesn't fit or make
much sense to me to lay
at God's feet all of
nature's fits & foibles...
all of humanity's
faintheartedness & failure.

Rather, I experience, know
God as an awareness of
the infinite in *us*...
                INCARNATION...
And if Jesus was fully human,
fully divine, so are we all,
aren't we? He was just better
at it...the divine more fully
realized and revealed in him
somehow.

Does that view make me
a heretic? Well, here I stand,
a fringe on the prayer shawl
of organized religion...
   unable, unwilling to
   force my way back
   into the orthodox center,
   yet also unable, unwilling
   to let go of my heritage...
   and so I h
            a
               n
                  g   on.

June 26

I thank You God for this most amazing
day: for the leaping greenly spirits of trees
and a blue true dream of sky, and for everything
which is natural which is infinite which is yes.
-e.e. cummings

BRACHOT - Hebrew blessings

Blessings said throughout the day,

Reaching out to touch & heal,
        hold & cherish.

Acknowledgments of those in need &
  all the needs of this poor world:
    violence, injustice, sickness & war-

Compassion taking wing and dwelling
  in your human form,

Heart touching heart, when hand
  cannot reach; holiness enfleshed
  in each breath & blessing,

Outpouring of love, of loving concern,
  of deep involvement in this
  daily life,

Touching the earth,
  touching the sky,
  touching the other...
    making connections.

June 27

psalm of the breaking-open heart

What is causing my heart
to break wide open?
  The pain I see & hear
    around me...
  the need & struggle &
    frustration of so many...
  scenes of war, famine, & flood...
    dying children, grieving parents,
      dying species...

rampant disregard for
the life of Planet Earth.
So, to what are you calling me,
Divine Spirit? What am I to do?
I cannot do everything,
but I can do *one* thing!
Do not let my fears immobilize me-
fear of failure
fear of the opinions of others
fear that my little bit will
mean nothing in the grand
scheme of things
You have looked into my heart...
you know me more fully
than I know myself.
Grant me the wisdom
the insight
the honesty
to answer your call
to go deep...and to emerge breathless,
dripping in the waters
of rebirth
of truth
of holiness & wholeness,
alive with purpose...
enlivened with direction...

*Only hope can give us the courage to face the future and to stand
deeply in the present without running from it.*
-Matthew Fox

reflections...

June 28

We hold what we can.
The rest we let go.
-Karah G. Fisher

saving time

How do we "save time"?
Can we store up
   what we save and use it
   when time is short?
We crowd our lives with
"time-saving" devices which
take our time in learning how to
use them...and take *more* time
to earn the money needed for
their purchase...in order to do what exactly?
Where is the Time Bank
in which we can make
deposits of time saved...
            minutes earned?
Can "Saved Time" be tacked on
at the end of this life,
   to give us extra days
               or weeks
               or months
               or years of life?
Or is it simply an illusion,
   this thing of saving time-
   when what we really need is
   to live fully- every moment
               every hour
   aware that time is short
      and waits for no one
      and life- this life-
      is what we have
         at this point
            in time.

164.

June 29

*Some of us- perhaps ALL of us- have come to know the darkness
intimately and have found, much to our surprise, that hope lives there.*

for Sally & Mark...and me
in darkness is growth
there the seed lies buried
readied for new life

in darkness is truth
dying precedes living
new life comes from death

in darkness is hope
pain is not the last word
soon the light will dawn

June 30

*Everything has something to teach us. The only question is,
Do we allow it, or do we resist it with all our might?*
-Joan Chittister

ahead
Ahead of me lies
a day...
   fraught with possibilities...
and I face it
filled with joy-
      at being alive
      at being able to read & think
      at having a safe & comfortable home
      at being healthy as I near sixty-six
      at having an amazing panoply
             of friends & family
I breathe in
the holiness of this moment-
    and cherish the gift.
My prayers for the day?
   to not miss a moment of grace
   to live in awareness
   to celebrate life. IT IS ENOUGH.

165.

JULY-
long, hot summer

July 1

Summer is not, I must confess, my favorite season. The heat drains my energy, my initiative, my creativity, leaving me wrung out and cranky. But the natural world has a wonderful way of coping...of being...in spite of the circumstances, and butterflies brighten our world, regardless of the weather...as they ARE what they are intended to be, doing the task for which they were created. I have a lot to learn...and these beautiful, ethereal creatures have much to teach me.

fluttering by

Stifling heat...
air thick with humidity...
my body in rebellion
   from the contrast between
   the air-conditioned
       inside & the
       heavy yet more real
            outside.
On the other side of the
tightly-closed French doors,
   butterflies, oblivious to my
   human discomfort, flit from
   flower to flower,
      pausing only to
        extract the sweetness
        from the beauty I see-
          from a distance-
      seemingly aware
      that the nectar is their
        their life's blood...
      that sucking up
         life's essence grants
         them their brief but
         breath-takingly beautiful
         span of life...
    while here I sit,
    holding life's beauty
        at arm's length...
        complaining all the while
        about the heat...

168.

July 2

life goes on...
Sometimes I wonder just
how my life has brought me
to this *shape*...this visage.
   Gazing at the aging face
   in the mirror- *MY* FACE!-
   I wonder how the lines have
   happened, how the sags & bags
   have formed, when inside, I
   still feel so young!
   Gazing at another woman
   at the mall or in the supermarket,
   I wonder how old she is...
      are we age-contemporaries,
      she & I? and do I look as old
      to her as she looks to me?
Sometimes I wonder, too, how long
I have to be & grow & do...
and think of those already gone...
   the ones untimely dead...
      where are they now?
   The life force which burned in
   them so brightly must live on...
         somewhere, somehow still alive,
         more than just a flicker
                  a burning ember.
Sometimes I wonder if I write
to leave a piece of myself behond...
   so I will not just fade away
                  be lost...
   that old, old fear of being no more...
In reality, I can do nothing about
aging & death, but I can write my life...
         my thoughts...my hopes...
         my dreams...and so, live on.

*To learn to know one's self, to pursue the avenues of self-development,
that's what I call creative aging.* -Ada Barnett Stough

July 3

Life is not always what one wants it to be, but to make the best of it as it is, is the only way of being happy. -**Jennie Churchill**

angel unawares

Fly swatters- she was holding
a colorful bouquet of fly swatters-
nearly 2 dozen- and unable to resist,
I remarked,"You must have a lot of flies!"
"Oh," she replied with a smile,
"I work in a nursing home, rather
old and rundown, and there are
always flies- and I just thought-
well, every room should have a
fly swatter...it's only right."
And as we waited together
in the line at Walgreens',
she told me of the people
there- many quadriplegic,
she said, and young...
she was a physical therapist,
she said, and did what
she could. There wasn't much
money for frills, she said, but
every room should have a fly
swatter...at least that.
Her short halo of golden
curls gave light to her
open, ordinary face-
her eyes shone with the
compassion of this simple
act...and spontaneously,
I hugged her. "Thank you," I said,
"for being an angel to those
people today." And for a moment,
just a moment, we held & clung to
one another, sisters of the heart,
brought together by a colorful
fly swatter bouquet.

170.

July 4

In this day and time when, to question or disagree with our government is to be considered 'unpatriotic', I often find myself feeling out of step with many of my fellow Americans...especially on Independence Day.

independence day

How do I celebrate freedom when
so many in our world are imprisoned-
> in poverty
> in starvation
> in illness
> within actual prison walls
> in mental illness
> by governments which take & do not give
> by injustice and greed
> by circumstances beyond their control?
How do I justify the millions spent on
> fireworks throughout this land? on
> firefights in distant lands? while
> down the street or just across town,
> children go to bed hungry, elders
> are forced to choose between medicine
> and food...men & women maimed
> by war's insanity fight here for
> life & dignity...
>> while parades & concerts &
>> speeches laud & celebrate the
>> Land of the Free and the Home
>> of the Brave.
Don't get me wrong-
I love this nation...this place of
possibility and hope and freedom-
but until that freedom extends
to ALL, regardless of race or creed,
gender or sexuality, age or income
or status,
> I will weep this day,
> and pray my tears will
> wash away my shame & pain,
> my collusion & participation
> as a citizen of this land.

171.

July 5

beach clouds

Clouds
   great billowing storm clouds
   covering the upper reaches
     of the sky
   with a racing layer below...
     dark gray & moving at a
     determined clip...with some
     great destination in mind...
And a scant thirty minutes
   later, puffy, white cumuli
     dotting an azure sky,
   the storm clouds fading away
     to the south...total transformation
         prestidigitation
            before my very eyes...

July 6

the day begins...

Help me to stride **boldly** into the day, O Christ.
Let me draw the strength I need.
Let me be true to you, to my self, to my calling.
Open my mind & heart
   and clear away the fear.
Grant me the gift of
   overwhelming peace...
     may I find there my
     rest & my salvation...
Set me free from my own rigidity...
     and open me to learn from
     those with whom I disagree...
Grant me boldness &
     bravery without brashness...
Shape my words with
     wisdom & compassion. Let it be so.

July 7

perspectives

We each "see" the world
from our own
     perspectives...
from the many "places"
    we have stood...
    the myriad of roles
    we have played.
My view, of necessity,
differs from yours,
  even as my life experiences
  have been different
        from yours.
So what are *my* perspectives?
  Mother...sister...daughter...
  grandmother...friend...caregiver...
  nurse...hospice director...pastor...
  reader...writer...poet...aging woman...
  single person/married person/widow/divorcee...
  survivor- of the death of a husband,
      a sister, a child, & cancer.
Each one a pane in the window
  through which I view
    the world...
each one a facet of the jewel
    I call "my life".

reflections...

July 8

in the Charlotte railroad station
(to the young black woman sitting next to me)

I live inside a white skin.
I guess that makes me "white"- though I'd
   rather think that who I am is
      more than skin deep...
      more than graying hair
        and wrinkling face.
For if you take the time to LOOK
   at me,
      I hope the shade of skin or hair
      is last and least
        of what you see...
      for buried here
      within the depths of
        who I am
           is humor, intelligence &
                    wit...
      a mind that questions still,
      that gasps & grasps with glee
        at new discoveries...
I don't know how to be
another me-
   and cannot change my
   skin or age-
      and will not change my hair!
Don't let those things
   separate us, please.
      See me for ALL of who I am
      so that I can see you,
             too...

You have to leave the city of your comfort and go into the wilderness
of your intuition. What you'll discover will be wonderful.
What you'll discover will be yourself.
-Alan Alda

174.

July 9

Retirement was the destination I reached after a long and often-agonizing journey of discernment. Practicality said NO; but my heart said YES! After thirty-one years of being responsible to someone else for the product of my labors, I needed to be responsible only to myself. Writing called...and though I deeply and profoundly admire those who write with children crawling around their feet, with laundry & dishes & cooking to be done, that has not been possible for me. The delight of retirement- even as I occasionally work part-time- continues to be a gift I cherish each day. And I write!

retired...

Retired...letting go of what has been...
allowing yourself to be
re-shaped
re-newed
re-born
walking through the passageway
from what you *have been* doing
to what you want to do & be
here & now!
Taking time to
rediscover your self...
who you have become
in the passing years &
who you still want to be...
Not governed by time &
schedules...
perhaps for the very first time...
time taking on a
different meaning...
in some ways, more precious-
in some ways, less important-
but with the sure & certain
knowledge that it will not
stretch on forever...
but, oh, the sweet
sublimity of what
is left-
and the delicious
mystery of not knowing
what comes next.

*We do not know the beginning
Or the end
We only see the middle of things
Which is our own life.*
-Alice Walker

175.

July 10

memories

Memories of childhood-
summer evenings playing
in the neighborhood- and
inevitably, the call would come-
    "Linda! Lin-da! Time to come in!"
And the temptation always- to stay for
just one more game of "Red Rover",
to catch one more lightning bug...
to ignore the call...deny even hearing it...
But I knew the call would not
go away...would come again,
more persistently, with greater
intensity- and there *would* be
consequences if I didn't respond...
So I dragged myself home...
oh-so-reluctantly responding
to Mom or Dad, looking longingly over
my shoulder at friends who could
stay outside a little longer...
    wanting to join them, even as I was
    yawning, my eyes barely able to stay open.

Fretful child of God that I am,
I *still* often respond with reluctance,
don't I? Pretend not to hear the voice
so I can do my own thing just a little longer...
    unwilling to admit that, left
    to my own devices, I would *not*
    become all I have been created to be.
Even when my eyes are drooping,
I am reluctant to acknowledge
    my need for rest;
even when my heart is achingly lonely,
I often resist admitting my need for
    community & connection;
even when my calendar is full,
I hesitate to recognize the need for
    simplifying & prioritizing.

Thank you for your patience
        with me, Mother/Father God.
Thank you for lovingly leading, guiding,
                        calling, prodding
even when I want to stay outside,
playing my *own* games. Help me
to realize that what you offer is
the real joy of freedom...growth...service.
Instead of catching fireflies &
putting them in jars, you call me
to help light up the world with
    the wonder of your beauty...
            to BE- with you-
                the Light of the World.

July 11

The spiritual quest, seeking to learn about the Divine and how divinity is revealed in this world, continues to be one of the most important parts of my life. And over the years, beginning in my early teens and continuing into the present, orthodoxy- right doctrine- has become less & less important, while the experience of the Incarnate God in my life has become the ground on which I stand.

TAPROOT

I need to be
    rooted in something...
    to stand on something-
        other than my
                own self...
a place
a source from which
    I can draw strength
                wisdom
                energy
                courage
Traditional God-language
causes me to cringe...
    lacks the ability to
    help me see &
            know God...
                that essential truth I seek.

I revel in ritual...a signpost
pointing to & acknowledging
    some larger truth &
            presence & reality...
but orthodoxy...
  "right doctrine"-
    for its own sake
    holds no resonance
    within my heart & soul.
I stand on the Ground of Being,
letting the winds of the Spirit
blow through my hair & heart & mind...
            and truth is revealed!

There is at the heart of
the gospel a call to radical insecurity.
-Anthony Freeman

July 12

explaining God
What do I mean
when I say
  I believe in God?
Who/how/what is
  God to me?
        a force...
        an energy...
        a link...
        a connection...
        the spark of life...
        a well-spring from which
            all good flows...
        the source of
            all love...
        a god of my own creation?
But from where else
could my image
of God come
    but within me?
  from my imagination,

my creativity...
        not outside but inside...
        yet also around &
                with &
                under...
I sense something *beyond* me...
    and I call that Beyond "God".

July 13

Every single creature is full of God and is a book
about God. -**Meister Eckhart**

daily music

With windows open wide,
I am surrounded by
        immersed in
    a gentle cacophony
        of birdsong,
    the multiplicity of voices
        writing an early-morning
        symphony on the
        heavy air.
Wren, robin, towhee, cardinal,
finch, bluebird-
    each voice distinct
    and yet a complement to
        all the others...
    a rising chorus in
    anticipation of the
        rising sun-
    and the rising of one
    human creature-
        with tousled hair and
        sleep-stiff body-
    listening with deep
    appreciation to the
        gift of a new day,
            begun amidst the
            music of life's
            daily celebration.

July 14

The Word is living, being, spirit, all verdant greening, all creativity.
This Word manifests itself in every creature.
-Hildegard of Bingen

God calling...

I am here in the darkness...
feel enfolded, comforted, secure...
The pain in your heart
   comes from dissatisfaction...
             disconnectedness...
Let the light in.
Let me take you to a
   place of truth.
I hold your heart in
   my hand- I cherish it.
In me, you live & move & have your being.
I surround & fill you.
I am part of the paradox of life.
   Be complete.
   Be full.
   Be whole.
You can walk the Divine Path
   without fear for
   I walk with you...
      This is the truth.
      Surrender...
         let love emerge...
         it is enough.

July 15

prayer

I believe in, dwell in
   the "I don't know"
      of prayer...
unsure of how it works
     or why it works
      but
somehow convinced that
     it DOES work...

not because my entreaties
impact a Great Divinity,
but perhaps because
in opening my awareness
            to needs & problems &
                    hurting people,
        I allow them to impact *me*...
            to draw me in...
            to change me...
            to invite me to
                    acknowledge &
                    share in the
                    connection...
            to pick up my piece of
                    the pain of the world...
            to participate actively in
                    the divinity in all humanity...
                            and so I pray.

July 16
*I was taking a class on Spiritual Activism, part of a diverse group, each with
opinions to express, ideas stimulated by the weekly assigned readings. It
was exciting, challenging...but at times, I found myself saying too much...
expressing my own opinions with too much energy, perhaps preventing
others from putting forth their impressions and ideas. Mea culpa...*

listen!
Sometimes I talk too much...
express myself too passionately
and not well enough, without
sufficient forethought.

Be the guardian of my mouth,
O God, the filter for my words.
There is more to being present than
to express one's own opinion...it's
just that my mind races & I make
so many internal connections...

Restrain me, Spirit of Truth...open
my ears to LISTEN...*really* listen...

to be present without feeling
that I *have* to speak, *have* to respond...
mine is not the only opinion
in the room. Help me not to
forget that.

July 17

morning prayer III

Open my heart &
open my life this day.
I feel clenched inside...
   a tight fist of anguish
   and uncertainty,
   coming from- where?
           what?
           why?
       I do not know.
Perhaps I am simply carrying
a piece of the world's anguish...
   but perhaps I am
   clutching at control...
   at my need to be
   in charge of what happens-
          in my life
          in my world!
Is it possible, Brother Christ,
to take this whole responsibility
thing a bit too far? For when I feel
responsible, the onus is for me to
take charge...come up with
solutions...make "it" work-
       whatever "it" is.
Let my prayer rise before
you like incense, Holy One.
Create in me an open heart...
         open hands...
       an open life...

Help me to unclench the anguish...
the anxiety...the sadness...the need
to control...and let me rest today in
　　　your mothering arms,
　　　　wholly & surely held...
　　　　　　　　　　accepted...
　　　　　　　　　loved...just as I am. Amen & amen

July 18

flavorful

If all of life is gift, then even
all the musts & shoulds,
the to-do lists, the daily chores-
　like scrubbing the toilet
　　　cooking dinner
　　　watering the flowers
　　　emptying the compost bin
　　　　　　　　　are gifts.
They make up, take up,
　　　　moments of my life...
　　　moments to be valued...
　　　moments to be savored
　　　　　the way I savor the flavor of chocolate
　　　　　pecan ice cream on my tongue...
Admittedly, some are less
　flavorful and please my palate less,
　but the tastes of summertime
　are so varied and so glorious-
　　　　succulent peaches
　　　　juicy tomatoes
　　　　tangy blueberries
　　　　mouth-watering cantelopes
　　　　sun-ripened watermelons
　　　　and always, ever, ice cream,
　　　　the flavors many & varied
And like the daily tasks which
fill my day, I can savor the flavors
they bring and so give thanks-
　　　　　　for my life.　　　　　　183.

July 19

morning thanks

Awake!
Aware!
Appreciative!
   Thankful for this creation...
      for birds singing & sun shining...
      for the water which will soon
         shower me...
      for the food which will feed my body...
      for the people who will populate
         my day...
      for the ability to walk, think,
         speak, feel, see, hear, taste...
      for music & books & art...
      for ceiling fans & comfortable beds &
         lovely old houses...
      for my precious family...
      for beloved friends...
May today be spent in openness,
                  in awareness.
May I be fully present
                  in every moment.

July 20

numbers

We have difficulty
conceptualizing vastness-
whether of geography
        or space
        or numbers of children
            dying of hunger each day...
In an attempt to get our minds around
size, we make comparisons-
  like the size of Rhode Island
              OR
  the number of people
  living in Charlotte-

but I cannot *begin*
to picture, to comprehend,
   the number of people
   living in Charlotte
          OR
   the actual size of
   Rhode Island- can you?
And how, then, do we make sense
of the vastness of space
or weigh the impact of the
numbers of children
         dying daily?

July 21

skyward

We look up to see the sky...
forgetting that sky begins
where earth ends...
that any time
we venture out,
we are standing in
     surrounded by
       the sky!
Easier to see & experience in
   some places, of course-
for here at home, when I look up,
I see instead a canopy of green...
   the trees whose reaching arms
   provide shade & sustenance
   for all manner of
     earth's creatures...
They lift & nourish me...
remind me of the
vital truth of roots & reach...
      but sometimes-
      I need
        a different immensity.

July 22

possibility

This morning my life feels
fraught with possibilities.
I have this amazing
sense of YES!
>a deep certainty that the
>flow of my life is sure & true
>and will take me to
>amazing places in the coming days
>>>weeks
>>>months
>as I float bouyantly in a stream
>feeding into the joyously flowing
>river of my creative energy.

Don't ask me why or how
I know this-
>I just do!

And the music plays...
the coffee cools & yet warms me...
the delicate golden fairy
>floating from the head
>of my bed smiles her
>encouragement-
>>and another day
>>has begun.

reflections...

186.

July 23

Everyone's life is mysterious, beautiful,stunning magic. –Leslea Newman

hermetically sealed

Windows tightly closed...
nature held at arm's length-
or at least separated by a
pane of tempered glass from
where I sit, coffee cup in hand,
straining to hear the song of birds,
the sound of life *outside* my windows...
those things which offer connection
to the greater world...which draw me
out of this tiny sphere of "home",
this tiny space of "self"...to
where I *need* to be... engaged
                involved in more
                than just doing laundry &
                preparing meals &
                sorting mail &
                paying bills.
Those morning sounds draw me
out into the world...open mind & heart
to people and events beyond this
hermetically sealed structure where I abide...
        to hear the call
           to fast for hunger's sake...
        to weep for the
           passing of Pavarotti
           from the stage of life...
        to write to my
           congressman about
           the war...
        to step <u>out</u>...
        to leave the box...
        to be IN the world...
                alive
                aware
                engaged.

July 24

sunrise

Sun rising...
day beginning...
    praise & thanksgiving
    even in pain's midst.
Being human...
making choices...
    wisdom & courage
    to face the day.
God present...
God loving...
    hope & forgiveness
    filling my soul.

God is an ever-receding horizon calling us to endless possibility.
-Anonymous

sunset

Fairies dwell in the realm
  of Imagination...
they inhabit the corridors
  of Joy & Creativity...
they burst into life
  when we free them from
  the restrictive prisons
  of Reason & Logic...
They fly on gossamer wings
  through the shimmering
  twilight, sprinkling fairy
  dust on the dusty, weary
  world, transforming it
  into burnished gold for
      a brief, breath-held
      moment.

July 25

Sometimes I am afraid. I don't enjoy admitting this, not even to myself, but it is the truth. What I have found- over & over again- is that most often fear comes from inside rather than from any outside threat...and I can smile as I picture Debroah Kerr singing and whistling to her 'son' in "The King and I"... I LOVE to whistle!

fear's paradox

I have been avoiding & evading...
   out of brokenness & fear.
I am so much more
   fear-filled than I like
   to acknowledge...
so many things intimidate me-
   but when I finally face them,
   they melt away.
Honesty feels good...
   though there is still a
   place of trembling
   inside me.
But I have learned to live
with this inner "jelly"...
   I find that when I act
   bravely, I *become* brave...
   when I "whistle a happy tune",
   I become what I think
   I cannot be...by *being* it...
         a wholly holy paradox...
       and my heart gives
        thanks.

July 26

conflicting claims

There are conflicting claims
within me...my unity
is not complete...I am   far
from you, God-Spirit...
my mind & heart & sense of purpose
are not clear...unified...

Yet I know I am being led...
    have always known that...
    have always had a vision of holiness...
                    of whole-ness...
        motherhood...nursing...ministry...
        nurturer...pastor...shepherd
            the connections are many,
            the links are clear-
                perhaps more unity
                than I usually
                    recognize...
                    acknowledge...
Perhaps I complicate things
because the call is so clear-
        and I fight against it.
If I remain stuck in discernment,
                in searching,
        I can also stay stuck in
                    inactivity.
        Reflection is vital...but so is action!
Balance...wholeness...unity!
        It is my divided self
        that keeps me paralyzed.
Purpose, Gentle Spirit, purpose &
                    vision &
                    continuity...
                    openness &
                    willingness...
    to be pastor, to be mother,
    to be daughter, to be writer,
    to be prophet, to be friend...
    to be servant.
Help me to become unstuck...
        to become one
            with you & my world...
            today & every day.

One's purpose is a matter of knowing where one's talents
and the needs of the world intersect.
-Aristotle

July 27
Some mornings words will not come but sometimes, there is an embarassment of riches!

two morning prayers
Be with me today, Creative Spirit,
as I do those things
which my day requires
of me. Let the prayer of
my living rise before you
like incense...with an awareness
that this is a day of my
life passing by...a gift passed
from you to me & back again...
and on & out into my life...
May my ripple on the
ocean of the world reach a
distant shore & touch
someone. Create in me an
open, loving heart, O God...
and renew in me a spirit
of compassion & involvement &
concern for this planet
of which I am a part.
Let it be so. Amen

Guide my steps this
day, God of Grace.
Open my heart. Grant me
holy words & holy
thoughts. Bless all I love &
all I need to love...all
those needing your care &
compassion and all those
needing mine. Let it be so.
Amen

July 28

There are moments when the soul takes wings.
What it has to remember, it remembers;
what it loves, it loves still more;
what it longs for, to that it flies.
-Fiona MacLeod

beggar's bowl

The words of a Christian writer
return from years ago- "The Holy
Spirit can only fill the emptied heart."
And now words from a Zen master-
"Only when you are empty will
there be room for more knowledge
to come in."
   Different traditions voicing
   the same concept...Holy Creativity
   giving birth in many ways,
   her children of every shade & clime
   embodying the timeless truths
   of earthly life...connected by the
   common bond of holiness embodied...
      alive in every leaf & flower...
      in pounding surf & blowing wind...
      in bird song & in lion's roar...
      in a baby's cry & children's laughter...
      reflected within a lover's eyes
      and still aglow in the
      aging & ageless beauty
      of the very old.
With empty hands we enter life...
with empty hands we leave...
   and in between,
   the gift of emptiness
   keeps us true to who we are-
      willing to be filled
      willing to be emptied yet again...
         a beggar's bowl of blessing
           and being blessed.

July 29

We are not human beings making a spiritual journey...
we are spiritual beings making a human journey.
-Pierre Teilhard de Chardin

sabbath day

The day begins...
the Sabbath...
a day of rest, of letting in
what is too often held at
arm's length...an opening
of what is most often closed...
the heart, mind, life...
the threads of who we are
intricately woven in such
a way that they cannot
be pulled apart. Though we
fear it, unraveling does not
happen...only our perception
of it. Life IS...we ARE- for now-
and only now.

Ephemera...a passing
wisp of cloud...mixed
metaphors...seeming
paradox...yet such is life...
at the same time an
intricate weaving,
textured and tangible
and yet moving on,
fleeting as clouds
across the summer sky.

Here & not here...
not & not now...
real & unreal...
mystery thrives...
as no explanation will
suffice...
only awe & gratitude.

July 30

*I love the concept of the day entering us even as we enter the day. As we stand at the edge of morning, may you enter the depth & breadth & width of these twenty-four hours you have been given, regardless of what they bring. May you feel **all** you are meant to feel, think thoughts which will enrich & encourage those around you, do those things which emerge from your creative nature to make this a more beautiful world.*

aurality

Sounds...
layer upon layer of sound...
    the whisper of rain
    the early-morning song of birds
    the far-away, haunting sound of
        a train's whistle
    the glorious & benedictory notes
        of 'Ave Maria' from the CD player
An aural collage
decorating the landscape
of my morning...
as I sit expectantly,
welcoming the gift of
a new day.

The notion of the day as a sacred place offers a lovely frame for the creativity that a day can bring. Your life becomes the shape of the days you inhabit. Days enter us.
-John O'Donohue

July 31

another sunrise

Day beginning...life calling...ordinary
tasks ahead...one foot in front of the
other...the dill grows tall...the sweet
basil proliferates...the oregano spreads
majestically...day lilies lift their faces
to the rising sun...the cardinals feed
their offspring...the overwhelming
green of summer hangs heavy in the
trees...and golden fingers of sunlight
reach across the landscape of my
very own small place in the scheme
of things.

        Good morning.

194.

AUGUST -
the 'dog' days

August 1

The most important function of art and science is to awaken the cosmic religious feeling and keep it alive. -**Albert Einstein**

another day

Holy breath stirs
The trees...a cardinal
Sings his early-morning
Song, joyous to my
Listening ears...music
From the CD player fills
My room with healing
Sound...outside green abounds
As grasses, trees, weeds burst
Forth in the creative energy of
Generativity...and this artist,
this writer savors the touch of
Breeze on my skin...the sounds of
Inner and outer music on my ears...
Opening myself to the wondrous
Powers of creation, of
Creativity... In-breathed
                In-spired
                In-filled

August 2

blessing

Bless this day,
O God who is Here & Not Here.
Breathe into me the energy & creativity
    I need... the peace & loving concern...
Be thou my vision...
        the hope of my heart.
Help my wounds to heal...
repair the breaks in my
        fragile heart...
and set me on the way
        of peace. It is enough.
                For today, IT IS ENOUGH.
196.

August 3

shadow side
There she is...
hiding in the shadows...
      the "me" nobody else knows...
      the "me" I keep hidden
          lest her revelation
          cause others to
          turn away-   in disgust
                        in derision
                        in disappointment.
But she needs *my* acceptance...
        my loving compassion...
        my open forgiveness...
          if "she" is to live
               in the light.
Can I embrace "her"?
acknowledge & welcome "her"?
   realizing that only
   when I admit we are ONE
        will I ever be whole.

August 4
I continue to struggle with the conflict between orthodoxy and my own inner knowledge, walking the razor's edge of belief, at times feeling totally out of balance, but always seeking, searching.

gnosis
we only genuinely KNOW what
we have personally gathered
through our senses...
   all else is secondhand...
   hearsay evidence...
and if this is so- and I believe
it is- it means that in the realm
of faith/religion/belief, i trust
most what i KNOW...
   what i have experienced
   of the Divine...

In the end, the hole in the soul is not filled by answers. It is healed only by deeper questions.
-Alan Jones

far more than what the
church or any authority
tells me.
scholarly testimony,
tradition, have their place,
especially as a source of
comfort & security...
but the measuring stick
that i hold up to all i read
and hear and am told is
my own deep, inner 'sense'...
the knowing that comes
from the Unknown...
the seeing that reveals
the Unseen...
so what heresy am
i guilty of now?

August 5

*The spiritual life is seeded in darkness and ends in light. It is about
love, not law; it is about grace and energy, the cosmos and creation.
It is about hope at the edge of despair and a beginning where only the
end seems to be. It is about dailiness raised to the level of the ultimate
assurance that God is with us. It is only up to us to be with God.*
-Joan Chittister

getting lost

Somehow, O God, I have lost my way...
or at least, I seem to have strayed
from the path proscribed by my church.
The signposts & landmarks to
which they point seem to me
written in an unknown tongue...
scribed in a way which makes no sense
nor rings of truth...and following
them no longer seems an option for
this heartsick pilgrim.
Lost in the wilderness, blind &
hungry, I feel my way, groping along
in the darkness, praying, hoping for light...
but the silence rings loud, the darkness

only deepens, as I follow the trail of my tears.
O God, why have you forsaken me?
Or have I simply lost sight of you
in the never-ending mists of conflict
when the path had seemed so clear? so true?
Re-open my eyes, Healing Spirit.
Clarify my heart, Spirit of Truth.
Grant me courage, Holy One,
to step once again into the light and
to live with integrity, no matter what
voices mutter around me.
For you, Living Christ,
are the Truth
the Way
the Light in the darkness.
In you, I live & move &
have my being.
Amen & amen

August 6

transformation

To live in rhythm with
the flow of seasons,
the flow of what the body needs,
requires reflection...
and reverence for
the gifts of Mother Nature,
Mother Earth.
There is a time of fullness & abundance
and a time of seeking refuge...
of fallowness & rest
to permit healing & renewal...
a time when restoration happens...
and when the realization comes,
like the dawning of a new day,
that you are whole and
filled with creativity
once more.

199.

August 7

who I really am

I am
    an intelligent woman
        with strong intuition...
I am
    creative-
        in my expression
        in my view of life...
I am
    a good mother
    a great friend...
I am
    open to new ideas
        to change...
I am
    making the world
    around me a
        more beautiful place.
I am
    connected to
    all of life-
    and I care deeply
        for this planet
        on which I live.

August 8

Art is order, made out of the chaos of life. -Saul Bellow

wild horses

Inspiration is a surprising
Visitor, creeping up on
Silent feet when least
Expected, and often hiding,
Just out of sight, in spite of
Invitation...urging...
Desperate desire.
She cannot, will not
Be forced or coerced,

Her wild & independent
Beauty tamed only fleetingly
As she permits…the untamed
Mustang of her energy cannot be
Bridled but- if one is daring,
Courageous, willing to take the risk-
She offers a wild, bareback
Ride of total, unfettered
Abandon…across the landscape of
Creativity…
And this rider
Can only hang on
And shout, Yippee!

August 9

In recent years, I have become interested in quantum physics, a great surprise to me since Physics was my least favorite subject in high school. But the work of John Polkinghorne and others have grasped my imagination as surely as the fiction of J.R.R.Tolkien and J.K.Rowling, stretching my world-view, challenging what I thought I knew, and opening me to possibilities beyond my wildest imaginings.

probability

Probability rather than
certainty governs
quantum reality…
     which leaves room
     for free will.
The Zeno effect,
in quantum mechanics,
says that if we hold
the same intention
over & over again
by posing the same question
to the universe,
     we *change* the
     quantum probability
     away from randomness.
       Is this, then,
         the power of prayer?

August 10

impermanence

Impermanence, says quantum theory,
means everything changes...
    at *every* moment *everything*
    is undergoing transformation.
I am no quantum physicist
and much of what they write & say
is well beyond my ken,
but doesn't this sense of
impermanence mean that
    everything is possible?
    that sadness & suffering *will* pass...
    problems & pain *will* end...
        and nothing can remain
        the same because *every*
        thing is influenced, impacted,
        by everything else.
            And isn't there a
            mysterious, beautiful
            hope in that?

August 11

It was the best of times, it was the worst of times. It was the age of wisdom, it was the age of foolishness. It was the epoch of belief, it was the epoch of incredulity. It was the season of light, it was the season of darkness.
-Charles Dickens

tunnel vision

When we are afraid,
our vision narrows.
The squint of fear
contracts what we can see
and we lose sight of
the whole, focusing our
attention on the source
of our fear.
And with this narrowed
visual field, the blinders
fear puts on our eyes,

we miss the rest of what
flows all around us...
unable as we are
to process what is
there because we
can see only what
is *here*...FEAR!

But deep within each one
of us there dwells a
light, a source of wisdom
and of truth...
call it what you will:
       intuition
       the voice of God
       beginner's mind
       inner knowing
and if we pay it heed,
if we will trust & let go,
the path will clear...
the answers come...
as fear's narrow view
gives way to the
wideness of the grace of God.

reflections...

August 12

*What we call the beginning is often the end and to make an end
is to make a beginning. The end is where we start from.*
-T.S. Eliot

change
Instead of living in a
newly-built brick house
high on a hill
　　OR
in a farmhouse built
two centuries ago by a
Quaker farmer in
Pennsylvania, my dwelling
place is a cottage on a quiet
city street in a mid-sized
city in the South.

Instead of life amidst
the daily flow of family
and friends, I must rely
on phone, email, and
snail mail to keep
connections strong,
while daily life moves
at a far different pace
than once it did...

I walk a different path
in a different place...
yet was this where
I have been headed
all along?
　　How much choice?
　　How much chance?
　　　But always,
　　　　ever,
　　　　　change...

204.

August 13

The highest form of bliss is living with a certain degree of folly.
-Desiderius Erasmus

riancy

Did you know that
the neuroplasticity of
the brain- the brain's
ability to make new
connections, and the
prime ingredient in
learning & being able
to learn- increases
markedly
  after SURPRISE!
  after LAUGHTER!
So- why is school so serious?
    so often unimaginative?
How often is laughter
heard in the halls of
nursing homes?
   And have *you* laughed today?

August 13

*Doubt and dedication often go hand in hand. And 'faith', crucially,
is not assenting intellectually to a series of doctrinal propositions;
it is living in conscious and rededicated relationship to God.*
-Annie Dillard

morning plea

My heart cries out,
Where are you, God?
My loved ones need
your healing presence-
the balm of your love
to soothe the aching
wounds which rend
their souls & minds &
    bodies.
Why do you seem so
distant? So far off?

And yet I know that you
live within each one of
us- in & around & through &
through. We are bathed in
the Fountain of Life which
is you...held safe in the
amniotic water which daily
gushes forth to birth us anew.

Open my heart, Mothering God...
my mind, my awareness.
Let me know your sustaining,
nurturing love again & again.
And lead me on the path of
healing & compassion
for those I love, for those
who hurt.

You are my Source,
the Ground on which I
stand secure. In you,
I live & move & have
my being. Amen & amen

August 15

rising day...

Sun rising...
Day beginning...
Praise & thanksgiving
Even in pain's midst.
Being human...
Making choices...
Wisdom & courage
To face the day.
God present...
God loving...
Hope & forgiveness
Filling my soul.

206.

August 16

The acrostic has been used since early times- in the Psalms, for example-
as a way of conveying an idea, an image, in a beautifully creative way.
Sometimes I find one emerging unbidden, always a most welcome surprise.

symbol

Shadowy...unclear, deliberately
          undefined,
Yet pointing beyond itself to
    something deeper, truer...
Mysterious & mystical,
    myth & meaning
    intertwined...
Beauty revealed in ways
    beyond reason,
Ordinary things transformed
    extraordinarily...
Lifting us into the realm
    of spirit
    of holiness
    of divinity.

August 17

day dawns

Now, at last, the sky lightens,
though it is cloud-shrouded...
a bit like my heart this morning...
    my mind
    my spirit.
But the persistent miracle, the truth
of existence, is that beyond the clouds,
the sun *is* shining...
   and the hope of my heart-
   that it will break through to light
   & enlighten my day. Let it be so,
   Light of Light...
     let it be so.

August 18

Today would have been the birthday of my husband, Carl. He died of acute leukemia in 1975, at the age of thirty-seven. Though many years have passed, if I permit my heart to feel it, the pain of that time of my life is very fresh. And the question I am left with, though surely unanswererable: what would my life be like if the past had been different? Futile speculation, of course, but occasionally, there it is.

untitled

Unbidden the tears come. A deep,
bottomless bereftness...for opportunities
lost, for my failure to appreciate what
I had when I had it...for letting time slip
through my fingers like sand. And regret
rears its ugly head- while outside my
window a full moon sinks slowly in the
West and I await the rising sun to herald
a new day begun.
  The tears continue...
  my heart is breaking...
  O God I so long for,
  walk with me today.
  Bind up my wounds...
  let me cherish every moment
  of this day...
  because it will never, ever
  come again.
But at *this* moment,
this very moment,
all I feel is grief
          sadness
          loneliness,
as I sit, caught between
setting moon & rising sun...
the already & not-yet...
and hold hope like a
fragile gift in my
trembling hands.

208.

August 19

You must have a place to which you can go in your heart,
your mind, or your house, almost every day, where you do not own
anyone and where no one owns you- a place that simply allows
for the blossoming of something new and promising.
-Joseph Campbell

inner welcome

There should be room
within the 'home' which
is your soul to shelter
ALL of who you are...
> your wild divinity
> your many selves, each
>> bringing its own unique
>> difference
> your inner 'enemies', able to
>> reveal to you- if you will
>> linger unafraid- some
>> truth about yourself.

It is here, within this room that
you can practice 'inner hospitality',
> welcoming the shy &
>> secret &
>> sacred self...
> getting to know her
>> as an intimate &
>> precious friend...
> bringing the seemingly
>> disparate elements of
>> who you are-
>> WHO YOU REALLY ARE-
>> into glorious harmony.

reflections...

August 20

a different vision

'Nerve-wracking people are
God-in-my-face...'
Out of the blue those
words came, unbidden.
Something I had read?
Something I had heard?
But there they were,
falling like petals
onto the surface of
a pond...floating gently
in view, inviting me to
be aware of their fragile
beauty...to contemplate
their tender truth...to face facts...

How easily I mouth
the words of inclusivity
          acceptance
            connectedness...
How readily affirm
the unity of humanity,
created one and all in
the image of divinity...

    Then real life happens...
    and I encounter that person
    who challenges every truth
    which I profess...who drives
    me to the very edge of
    reason...who persistently
    tests my patience and
    puts me in a corner with
    no escape...
    Can I look him in the eye?
    Can I look at her and see
        God-in-humanity
            in front of me?

210.

August 21

The term 'Wonderful Becoming' comes from the writings of Thich Nhat Hanh, one of my favorite 'teachers'. His gentle, welcoming spirit comes through in his writings, as he calls for loving care of this world and all of its peoples.

ecology

'And God said...'
    so it began...
    the 'Wonderful Becoming' of
    creation...
    whether by bang
          or whimper
          or word,
               it began...
And for all of the millennia
of time, over all the epochs
of life on this lovely blue
planet, it has continued...
until, at this beginning
of another age, another
stage of being in this
place, we hear the call-
   you & I-
to be a part of the
'Wonderful Becoming'-
to live as co-creators
with the Wholly Divine-
to enter the dance of creation
and keep it going- whirling
            twirling
          always alive
              for the coming generations.

All that you do now must be done in a sacred manner
And in celebration
"We are the ones we have been waiting for..."
-The Elders, Hopi Nation,Oraibi, Arizona

211.

August 22

the day begins...
Help me to stride boldly
   into the day, O Christ.
Let me draw the strength I need.
Let me be true to you
        to myself
        to my calling.
Open my mind & heart
   and clear away the fear.
Grant me the gift of
   overwhelming peace...
      may I find there my
      rest & salvation...
Set me free from my
   own rigidity...
      and open me to learn from
      those with whom I disagree...
Grant me boldness &
      bravery without
      brashness...
Shape my words with
   wisdom & compassion.
      Let it be so.

August 23

*Strength of heart comes from knowing that the pain that we each
must bear is part of the greater pain shared by all that lives.*
-Jack Kornfield

morning prayer IV
Not grasping,
but groping,
  I begin my
  morning prayer...
  letting my heart
  break open with
  the pain of the world...
  the pain in which I share...

Holy Mystery, ground of Being,
   I lay myself open,
   offer myself to be guided,
   to be used as an instrument
   in the healing of the world.
       My bit is small- but
       it IS my bit...
       as important as that
       of every other being
       who walks this planet,
           breathes the air,
           drinks the water,
           eats of its bounty.
Do not let the immensity
of the pain overwhelm me-
or the many others who
willingly shoulder this
task of healing...
   enable & enliven us
   with purpose & hope.
As this amazing, fragile planet
struggles to survive,
   let me be consciously
   part of the solution...
   as I myself struggle
   to live with integrity &
               gratitude &
               wonder &
               a deep sense of
                   my connection with
                   all of life.

reflections...

August 24

cell phones

There is a sense of
IMPORTANCE we
attach to busy-ness
in this culture. Why
else would people stand
in public places talking
on cell phones?
Once there were
phone booths- people
wanted privacy for
their conversations...
but now the message
we seem to want to
convey is, "Look at me-
at how important I am...
how busy...how necessary"
(to someone...*anyone*...)
    How childish!
    How sad! that our sense
    of worth & importance
    comes always from
    others. Is this saying,
    "I am not enough
    in myself."?
        I wonder...

August 25

We live in all we seek. -Annie Dillard

summer watermelons

Though I am sixty-six and
   gray and sporting wrinkles
  in abundance,
     I still want all the
     fullness & succulence
       of life...

the dripping, overflowing,
>   messy juciness
>   of life...
and though I cannot swallow
it whole,
>   I can take bite after
>   mouth-watering bite,
>   and as the juice runs
>   down my chin,
>   see just how far
>   I can spit the seeds.

August 26

I continue to be drawn to the words of indigenous peoples in every part of the world and this morning prayer from the Aboriginal people of Australia speaks from their heart to mine- and I hope, to yours.

Aboriginal morning greeting

Hello, Divine Oneness.
We are gathered here within You, this special group of
Your beings.
We thank You for this day.
We thank You for each other. I thank You for me.
We dedicate this day to the honor of Oneness.
We ask that everything we need be provided for us.
We ask that everything we do today, say today, or hear today
be only to the highest good, in my highest good, in the
highest good for all life everywhere throughout the universe.
End of message.

reflections...

August 27

breathing beauty

I breathe in the fragrant scent
of beauty, fill my lungs with the
tantalizing breath
of nature's loveliness
    An azure sky, down-filled
    clouds, leaves of endless
    shades of green, stirred
    by a summer's breeze
    while in the nearby valley
    flows a chortling stream,
And here I lie, stretched in
a hammock, itself stretched
between two towering trees
Is this contentment
I feel? and joy?
     and peace?
     and blessing?
       Ah, yes.

*Oh Lord, how shining and festive is
Your gift to us, if we
only look, and see.*
    -Mary Oliver

August 28

*When someone we know is hurting, suffering, we are often at a loss for words.
We want to help, to say something. But as I know from experience, frequently
what we say is not helpful, coming from our own discomfort. Perhaps this is
when we most need to walk in someone else's shoes- or at least TRY to.*

left hanging

HANG IN THERE!
    we speak these words like
    a mantra of encouragement,
    support, to someone struggling
    with a problem, a situation
    which taxes their resources
    and brings them to the
    brink of desperation...
HANG IN THERE!
    things will get better, we
    imply. This can't last forever-

this pain, this problem, this
agony threatening to tear you
apart, body from soul,
limb from limb...
HANG IN THERE!
while deep within a
voice is crying, "I just
can't do this anymore!"
Can't bear the pain...
can't face the agony
which doesn't seem to
let up or let go...
BUT
is HANGING IN THERE
always such a virtue?
and shouldn't letting go
be an option for each
one of us at some point
in time?

August 29

*I am circling around God, around the ancient tower, and I have been
circling for a thousand years, and I still don't know if I am a falcon,
or a storm, or a great song.*
-Ranier Maria Rilke

surreality

Some days my life feels
surreal...but I am living it
and that makes it my reality,
doesn't it? I try really hard
to "follow the path in front
of me"...but somehow, that
only seems like reality if
there IS a path...

What if you're hanging out
there in midair, at the end
of your proverbial rope? Is
that when "Let go" comes
into play? trusting that when

I fall, I will land on my feet-
or at least on something fairly
soft- so I can get up, perhaps
bruised & battered, and
FOLLOW THE PATH
    once again?

Talk about surreal! For how
many times in life have I done
just that- hung there at the end
of my rope with even that end
unraveling- and finally given up...
                let go...
        because there was
        no other choice.
            And is this cowardice
                or courage?
                or simply the
                    surreality of life?

August 30

*This, then, is salvation: when we marvel at the beauty of
created things and praise their beautiful Creator.*
-Meister Eckhart

needing space

In Hebrew, so I am told, one of
the earliest words for 'salvation'
is also the word for 'space'...
    So how have we made
    the road to salvation
    so narrow, so well-defined?
In order to grow,
        to become,
        to be transformed,
we need S   P   A   C   E
    both within & without...
we need companions who, in love &
        trust & compassion, both allow &
        encourage us to be & become who we are
                    meant to be...

to celebrate & cherish &
    preserve our *difference* as
    well as our oneness &
    connection to all that lives.
Perhaps we have so narrowed the road
  because conformity is comfortable...
  because difference is daunting...
  because answers are preferable to questions...
But then, where is room for
  the awesome, breath-stopping joy
  of mystery?
  the overwhelming, miraculous
  wonder of resurrection &
  new life?

August 31

My firstborn child, Carl, died while scuba diving in Mexico in 1993, at the age of twenty-eight. I had already experienced the death of a husband and the death of a beloved younger sister. Perhaps those losses had prepared me in some small way for this life-wracking pain...but I must confess, it never really goes away, this agony from the loss of a child.

today's memories

He would have
been forty-three,
my eldest son,
born in the wee hours
of this day,
all those many years
ago, to a frightened
young woman,
laboring alone
in the maternity ward
of an Army hospital.
It was the way in
those days- few
words of comfort
were offered though
drugs were...
my husband sent
home with the

words, "It'll be a while."
Long hours of
pain made worse
by lonely isolation
and a harried, unfeeling
nurse, who kept
covering me each time
I ejected the sheet,
my tiring body
sheathed in sweat
as it labored in
earnest to birth
this new life.
And in the way of
those days, he was
whisked away
after only a brief
glimpse assured me
he was healthy & well.
We met face to face,
body to body, mother
and child, several
hours later and, oh,
the joy that flooded
my heart as tears
coursed down my
cheeks, my hands
running over his
tiny body, counting
fingers & toes, touching
every bit of skin,
taking him into my
heart & life inch by
precious inch.
My son...my first-born..
and with the memory,
unbidden tears
course down my cheeks...
this time of grief, of
life untimely gone,
of flesh-of-my-flesh

torn away at
twenty-eight. He
would have been
forty-three today,
my eldest son, and
I miss him still. Part
of me has gone
with him, for what mother
could let her child
make that last
journey alone?

*The best proof we have of the hidden gift in every struggle
is the fact that we survived the last one.*
-Joan Chittister

reflections...

SEPTEMBER -
autumn's edge

September 1

autumn's edge

The bare, dark outlines of the tree
outside my window emerge from the
lightening sky, the branches shivering
a bit in the almost-autumn breeze
which also stirs the candle sitting
next to me, the flame dancing with joy
in this first intimation of the season
changing...a foretaste of the autumnal
feast to come...Nature clad in glorious
gaudiness, the trees displaying their
riotous colors against the azure of the
cloudless sky. The voice of the harbinger
of fall pierces the air with scarlet song-
the cardinal calling to his faithful mate
who replies with quiet chirps...and I
recall the redolent scent of yesterday's
cooking- apples becoming succulent
applesauce, laced with cinnamon,
to delight & nourish for days to come...
and a container of homemade
soup thawing in the sink- both
sure signs of summer's wane
and autumn's ascendancy.
After a long, hot summer,
I welcome Fall with open arms
and await the equinox with
joy & eager anticipation...
changing seasons reflecting a
changing life, the truth that
nothing remains the same and
death must happen for
new life to come again...
                and so, standing
                at the edge of autumn,
                        I go on.
224.

September 2

My son, Paul, came into our lives from the Dominican Republic; a tiny child with dark hair & eyes, so unlike my three blond, blue-eyed teenagers. But Carl, Hope & Mark welcomed him with open arms & hearts, and he quickly became 'little brother', an integral part of our family.

september day

My September Day, he called it,
my chosen child...the day
when he entered our lives,
arriving at this place so far
from 'home', a place with
   different sights &
   different sounds &
   different smells &
   different faces...
his own small face drawn with
fear & lined with tears. How
could a child of three begin
to understand that in this
distant land a new life would
happen? What had he left behind
of love & connections broken?
We could not know. He could not tell.
And how has that September Day
molded & shaped the man
he has become, here in this
place, so far away from 'home'?

September 3

one closet

Ah! I cleaned
one closet today...
just one...out of
the nine which
populate my house...
all of which *need*
cleaning out, re-ordering...
   and I cleaned one, put it in order.

The other eight remain
in glorious- or inglorious-
                        disarray.
But I find I am content
to let them wait until another day,
    reveling instead in a sense
            of *this* day's accomplishment
    and letting go of
    the need to do more.
            One lovely,
                clean,
                    ordered closet.
                        Ah! It *is* enough.

September 4

We are talking about God. What wonder is it that you do not understand?
If you understand, then it is not God.
-Saint Augustine

moon musings

Full moon...a glorious
reflection of the sun's light
on a lifeless piece of rock,
moving around our larger
piece of rock rotating on
its axis, following its course
around our life-giving star,
and all of it moving
through space to who-knows-where?
Who watches?
Who knows the course,
the trajectory, the destination?
Far too complex to be
mere chance, even the chance
of quarks & quirks...
and I bow my head & my heart &
my mind & my knee to the
Greater Immensity I call
GOD.

226.

September 5

God speaks...

God speaks-
  in the sound of rolling thunder
  in the early-morning warble
      of the wren
  in the delighted giggle of
      a baby playing with its toes
  in the quiet murmur of friends
      sharing life's secrets
  in the majestic & mysterious &
      melodic strains of Mozart & **Sondheim,**
      Joplin & McCartney
  in the insistent & persistent chant
      of Navajo shamans
  in the whirling dance of
      Sufi mystics
  in the quiet dedicated chant of Buddhist
      monks & nuns in Tibet & Burma
  in the taste of shared bread & wine
      in Christian worship
  in the gentle thud of earth
      scattered on a coffin
God speaks in languages
many & varied...
          so how can we
          listen in only one?

September 6

heaven?

Where does the
life-energy go when
we breathe our last?
When the living
spark of consciousness
no longer glows with
sentient light?

The words I learned
so long ago in physics
class remain:
Energy can be neither
created nor destroyed;
it just changes form...
so what form will my
life-energy take when it
no longer enlivens this
mortal body? Where will
it go? How will it flow?
Is there a realm
of spirits made only
of energy & light?
And is this what
many call "heaven"?

September 7

Calmness of mind does not mean you should stop your activity.
Real calmness shoud be found in activity itself.
-Ram Dass

ordinary blessings

Today I made a pie...
  mixed & rolled the crust
  made the luscious filling
  put it in the oven
  and reveled in the
  fragrant scent of baking-
      of cinnamon & apples &
      pastry blended to
      create the smell of autumn...
Today I cooked a stew...
  chopped potatoes, onions,
  carrots, put them in the crock
  pot and spent the afternoon
  surrounded by the warm &
      welcome smell of supper cooking...
Today I ironed some linens...
  smoothed the wrinkles
  from napkins & tablecloths

& placemats which will
grace my table to welcome
guests and family alike,
the fragrance of fresh-pressed
cloth rising from
the ironing board to
blend work & pleasure
in a homely mix...
Today I did these simple tasks....
holy endeavors all...
and I received once again
the blessing of the
ordinary.

September 8

education

My favorite teacher from
the past was Mr.Goyt,
who taught by invitation,
creating in our classroom,
with his hospitable spirit,
a welcoming & daring place
of exploration and creation...
encouraging questions...
making us laugh...
and loving us into learning
because we loved him back.

My favorite recent teacher
is my grandson, Jamie, who,
with his loving and wide-open
heart, creates a place where
I can be a child again, open to
exploration and creation...
sharing questions, seeking answers...
doubling over with the laughter
caused by rampant silliness...
and loving me into being
more myself because we
love each other so much.

September 9

Sometimes the best way to deal with things which are stressing us out is to turn them on end, to see them from a different perspective. And by the way, STRESSED spelled backwards is DESSERTS! Surely that should tell us something important.

S-T-R-E-S-S

Did you ever
notice that
STRESS is,
   in another shape,
     RESTS?

Most of us, when
stress holds sway,
     grasps tightly,
     twists us out of shape,
   correct in the wrong
   direction...
       doing *more* instead
       of hearing STRESS
       as a signal to REST...
         to take little "Sabbath"
         times throughout our
         day- to breathe
            to laugh
            to nap
            to pray
            to give thanks for
        the "stuff" of life which
        gives it shape & substance-
          family & friends
          work & leisure
          body & spirit
          thinking & feeling-
   and *then* return again
   to life's demands,
     whole & renewed.

September 10

In one of those serendipities that punctuate life, I tuned in to NPR one afternoon in the middle of an interview with Irish mystic and poet, John O'Donohue. I was transfixed- by his voice, by his poetry, by his view of the world. Only at the end of the program did I learn he had recently died- but he has left an enchanting legacy of poems, prayers, and writings which speak to my heart at its deepest, truest place.

with gratitude to John O'Donohue

You are the only threshold
to your inner world.
By your words, your actions,
you reveal who you really are...
       how you see the world...
       what matters to you...
As you speak, as you live,
you bring sound out of silence...
    coax the invisibile to become
       visible...
You, me, each one of us
incredibly human creatures,
is making a life-journey
   of vulnerable complexity...
traveling a path of continual
   transformation...
     time veiled in eternity.
And at the heart of us-
each one of us-
    old, young
    male, female
    rich, poor
    gay, straight-
is an ancient namelessness...
   the abiding place of mystery,
   holiness...the unsayable, the
   ineffable...the Divine clothed
   in our human flesh.
And so, you, me, each one of us,
needs a companion on the road,
an Aman cara, a soul friend,
to whom you can reveal the deepest,
truest parts of yourself,

knowing they will be received
   with love, held with compassion,
   honored for their honesty,
   cherished for their immediacy.
It is for this intimacy that
every heart yearns,
every heart seeks...
      God with skin on
      living...enfleshed
            yet again- in us.

...the more you become sure of your own center,
the more you can also open your boundaries. -Richard Rohr

September 11

It was the fifth anniversary of September 11, 2001, and as I sat alone,
remembering, tears running down my cheeks, these words emerged.

remembering...

We hear & say the words
like a mantra-
            nine-eleven...
remembering the day
which changed us as
a nation...
            nine-eleven...
the day when fire & brimstone
rained down on Manhattan...on
Virginia...on a Pennsylvania field...
            nine-eleven...
and Evil reared its
gorgon head to spew the
filth of fear & hatred,
xenophobia & violence...
            nine-eleven...
the nations gathered 'round us then,
to comfort and to wipe our tears, as
grief & horror spread world-wide,
and people of goodwill reached out
to link their arms & hearts with ours...
            nine-eleven...

But that goodwill has fled as We,
the People, have abandoned Hope
to wear instead the mantle of Fear,
to arm ourselves with Violence,
to gird ourselves for War...
                    God of Peace, have mercy.
We focus all our attention on
the Enemy Without, and fail to
recognize & own & confess the
Enemy Within...
                    God of Grace, have mercy.
We continue on our common path
of overuse...of greed & grasping...
of selfishness & pride, closing our
collective eyes to the reality that
all around this globe we share
hunger, illness, inhumanity abound...
                    God of Justice, have mercy
We close our ears to cries of pain-
from a planet suffering the results of
overuse & abuse...from people being randomly
but systematically destroyed...from mothers
as they hold their dying children- in Darfur,
in Somalia, in Afghanistan, in Iraq, in
Chernobyl- while we drive in cars & fly
in planes in ever-increasing numbers...
                    God of Compassion, have mercy.
We justify our lack of doing something,
anything, to influence our government
run amok by saying, "I am only one...
what can I do? No one will listen anyway,"
while all around the world people
demonstrate against the very ones who
seem to rule our fate...
                    God of Courage, have mercy &
                    give us strength.
As today we remember those whose lives
were lost that fateful day which changed us
as a nation, let us pray again
for change...
        of heart & mind & purpose.

Let us confess our part
in this world's ills and
refuse to point the finger of blame
unless we also point it at
ourselves.
Let us renew our often-tenuous
connection 'to this world...grasp
tightly the delicate thread which
binds us to one another & to ALL
of God's created peoples, to God's
holy & beautiful creation,
mindful that we have been called to
be stewards & not consumers.

> God of All Creation,
> hear our prayer &
> give us purpose. LET IT BE SO.

September 12

I've known for some time that holding on to anything ruins it,
as does clinging to old way, outdated ideals, worn-out relationships,
and lifestyles that have run their course.
-Joan Anderson

out there...

There is a wisdom in knowing
when it is time to leave, to walk away,
a peculiar grace in knowing when
to say good-bye to a thing

> a person
> a job
> a belief
> a worldview

Often we stay, I think, because
to walk away is to disappoint someone
else...to have them think less of us...
   but what about disappointing yourself
   by not being true to your deepest truth?
Sometimes I stay where
I am- inside the walls of
this house I love- because
to venture out means taking

risks...allowing myself to be
vulnerable...open to
challenge & change.
> But I *need* the pull outward...
> the space of the wider world...
> the engagement in & by something
>> larger than myself...
> the sense that I have far to go
>> before I sleep.

September 13

worry

Worry accomplishes NOTHING...
> so says the Dalai Lama,
> echoing the voice of the Buddha,
>> the voice of Jesus,
>> the truth of all the ages & sages.

When pain or suffering
comes, then- and they *will* come-
> consider carefully whether
> there is anything you
> can do to change things...
>> if you can, DO IT...
>> if you cannot, LET IT GO...
>>> in either case,
>>> there is no need to worry.
>> The choice before you-
>>> to act or accept.

reflections...

September 14

pulled

I am feeling pulled apart...
my mind & heart going in
different   directions...
How do I unify my self?
How do I come to a place of one-ness
of body, mind & spirit?
How do I learn deeply?
care deeply?
work for justice deeply?
and still continue
the day-to-day tasks
of life which NEED to
be accomplished?
For who else will shop? cook?
pay bills? run errands?
make phone calls?
change the beds?
clean the bathroom?
do the dishes?
Who else will spend time with mother?
stay in touch with family & friends?
spend time in prayer?
Not to mention getting exercise...
eating mindfully & healthfully...
reducing stress...
And where is room for FUN?
PLAY?
simply BEING?
Wise & Compassionate Grandmother God,
slow me down today.
Help me to focus on one step,
one activity, one need at a time
Breathe into me an appreciation
for the moment,
for the tiny sabbath seconds which
dot my day- if I let them.
Open my eyes to the glory & fun
of simply LIVING...and help

me to see the every-day-ness
of my life as a precious gift in which
so many on this planet do not share.
May my day be punctuated
by laughter, delight...by the
willingness to be surprised by
simple things, blessed by the mundane.
And when at last I lie down
to sleep, grant me a grateful
heart, overflowing with the
moments of my day.
Amen & amen

September 15

*Hospitality...is a way of living from the heart and
extending the heart to the stranger.* -Frank MacEowen

coming home

I seek for a new homeland
in which my soul can dwell
for my remaining years...
a place of limitless possibility
where I can live in openness
and expectation...constructed
with flexible walls and countless
windows & doors so it will not
be too rigid,
  but welcoming & lovely.
Perhaps it needs to be a tent,
portable and far less permanent...
a tent of red, with flaps open wide
to catch the Spirit's breeze, with
mosquito netting flowing, to keep
out the pesky critters, with wind
chimes to sing the song of the wind...
  a place to welcome good friends-
      to talk & laugh & sing
      to celebrate life.
  A lovely vision- can I make it mine?

September 16

god talk

My personal theology is truly
an amalgam- born of experience and learning
of the daily journey
and occasional revelation.
My roots are deep within Christianity, but they
have grown and blossomed into an ever-diverse
expression of God with us
God IN us
God around us!
It is not about being *right,*
or having the *right* answers.
It is about finding my own way,
being a perpetual pilgrim
on the journey of life
and meeting many & varied
companions along the way.

September 17

gentle me, o God

Gentle me into the day, O God-
be my ever-present source.
Gentle me into the day, O God-
guide my often-faltering steps.
Gentle me into the day, O God-
fill my heart with gratitude & peace.
Gentle me into the day, O God-
open my arms to receive & accept
whatever comes.
Gentle me into the day, O God-
and when I come to its end, welcome me
into the arms of sleep, certain I have used
the gift of today wisely & well, blessing as I
have been blessed. Amen. Let it be so.

238.

September 18

May you have the wisdom to enter generously into
your own unease
To discover the new direction your longing wants
you to take.

-John O'Donohue

a blank page

The blank page stares at me...
  confronts & challenges me...
    "Fill me- I dare you!" it seems
    to say.
And the thoughts in my head
trip over one another as
they seek to be heard...
  "Me first!"..."no, me!"
  "I've been waiting for so long..."
    a cacophony of voices-
                silent voices-
                longing to be expressed-
                        by me.
And so, with pen in hand,
I make a start...a new beginning,
  with openness & honesty my goal...
I write to discover who I am...
                how I feel...
                my own voice...
        today it is a groan of pain...
            a shriek of agony...
        tomorrow-
          who knows?

reflections...

September 19

What would happen if one woman
told the truth about her life?
The world would split open.
-Muriel Rukeyser

the view from girlhood circa 1948

Daily the men left...
and the women cried- and lied ...
wept...and crept
lest they stepped
too heavily upon
someone else's toes.

Frozen smiles...
female wiles...
miles & miles of lies...
lies...
lies...

To be a woman meant
to live a lie...
to hide behind a mask-
of what?
satisfaction?
contentment?
surely not joy!

To trade intelligence and ability
and talent and curiosity, creativity
and inventiveness for security
and ordinariness and cookie-cutter
sameness and convention...
the only joy was to be a BOY-
or to *have* a boy...

September 20

*Discontent and disorder are signs
of energy and hope, not of despair.*
-Dame Cecily V. Wedgwood

chaos theory

CHAOS is the price of change...
    reigning for a time as
    old patterns are broken...
    old beliefs & ideas challenged...
    old paths disappear in the
      darkness of confusion.

CHAOS, a period of disorder,
    will happen when the
    old, familiar, safe is
    left behind and
    we careen along the
    road of life uncertain of
    direction or destination,
    seemingly at the mercy
    of this capricious,
    sometimes malicious imp
    who threatens our stability
      with unpredictability.

But behind the CHAOS- or
    from within its surprisingly
    tender grasp- new order
    comes, a new pattern
    emerges, life takes on
    a different shape, and
    we can see that CHAOS
    is not the enemy, but
    clears the way for
            new ideas
            new birth
            new life-
                as we begin again.

241.

September 21

Many writers, philosophers, spiritual seekers regard this time in which we are living as a pivotal, fertile time...a time filled with more & more people who are searching for truth & meaning, who are experiencing a deep connection with the earth, with all of nature, with one another. It is a holy time...and we are part of it- if we choose.

time after time

Once upon a time-
as archaeologists measure time
rather than fairy-tale time-
humankind honored the earth
as the Great Mother, felt
connected to & blessed
this source of life.
And 'women's work' was seen
as sacred: pottery & weaving
      grinding wheat & baking bread
      birthing & caring for children
   all sacred acts of worship,
   linked to the great creative
   work of Mother Earth herself.
Today- in the here & now of
measured time- much of
humankind seeks reconnection
with our Source- unraveling the
tapestry of misdirection woven
across the ages of time, reweaving
another with the threads of
partnership & love until we
understand again that the Sacred,
the Holy is present in the tasks
of every day and each one
we meet holds a Spark of
the Divine.

We are in the midst of the world's fastest transformation.
In times of major transformation, two things occur: a sense of breakdown,
a sense of possibility or breakthrough.
-Joan Chittister

242.

September 22

another morning blessing
O Spirit of Truth,
I relish the path I walk
as I seek the truth
of my own life.

I cherish my uniqueness...
my individual beauty
as well as my interconnectedness
with all life.

I am part of all on whom
I ask blessing, on whom
I shower light & energy & peace.

I connect with the people
of my life...my soul-links.
Cover them with love & light
this day, Spirit. Grant each one
the peace s/he most needs.
    And me also.
            Amen & amen

September 23
They pave the road to Hell, so it is said...yet good intentions are vital to
life. They serve as our guides, give us direction, define our purpose.

good intentions
"Set your intention..."
    so begins each
    yoga class...
        and breathing deeply,
        filling my lungs, my body
        with life-giving air, I set
        my intention for this day,
                        this life:
To keep growing
        searching
        exploring to the end of my days...

To enjoy every moment, regardless...

To be free of any fear, for
    fear inhibits, limits...

To honor my spiritual roots but to
    permit them to be re-formed
                re-shaped
                take on new meaning...

To love fully- first myself and
    then those who mean most
    to me and then the world...

To write my life, in whatever
    way it expresses itself,
    for that is how I speak
    my deep truth.

And as yoga molds, strengthens, re-shapes
    my body, may my intention do
    the same for my spirit...
                my life.
                Namaste.

September 24

an ordinary day
I enter the holiness of a day
well-begun. The breath of life,
of creativity, flows through me.
I am energized, alive,
    renewed by rest.
Outside, birds serenade
because they are birds.
And I begin to hear
human sounds:
    mother down in the kitchen
    a few cars on Sunset
    the echo of traffic on Main
    now a car beneath my window
        on Council

A door slams next door;
the rottweiler across the way
offers his morning 'woof'.
My day is fully & surely begun.
May I use it fully & wisely & well.
May I appreciate the ordinary.

September 25

The depths of our beings are not all sunlit; to see clearly,
we must be willing to dive into the dark, inner abyss and acknowledge
the creatures we may find there. **-Starhawk**

unseen

People in our lives, I have found,
  expect us to remain unchanged,
  to be our 'old selves'
  even after we have walked
  through the fire...
  even after life has left us
  battered & bruised & discarded
  at the side of the road...
      barely surviving
      hanging on by a thread...
  even after we have begun
  to heal and scars are forming
  at the broken places...
  and we are forever changed.
They- these people in our lives-
  often don't know what
  to do with who we have
  become...
  they find their status quo
  upset, askew...
  their plaintive cry
  resounds & echoes-
      'Why? Why can't you
      just be like you were?'
        nursing their own discomfort
        while we bleed out quietly
        from unseen wounds...

September 26

help!

Help, Healing Spirit!
I need your help today.
Enlighten this perpetually-
dark place in which I
find myself.

I cannot see the path-
though outdoors the sun
is shining.
　　　　Is this depression?
　　　　Nothing new at this
　　　　time of year...
　　　　but how do I hold
　　　　myself together?
　　　　With paper clips &
　　　　rubber bands...
　　　　with bandaids &
　　　　lots of tape...

but how do they help
when a heart is
breaking?

September 27

just wondering

Right now, I think
I would like to live
for a long, long time...
another twenty-five years
at least.

But will I feel differently
when I am mother's age?
When my friends are gone?
When I can no longer drive?
When life has been pared
down to the core of mere
existence and the 'world' has
shrunk to two or three
rooms on the same floor?
     I wonder...

And as we age, do we become
different people than once we were-
more fearful, pessimistic, depressed-
or are we simply distilled down
to our essence- whatever that
may be...our most essential,
truest self?
     I wonder...

For each passing day brings
me nearer to that time which
once seemed so far away...
and honesty requires me
to admit that far fewer
years remain than those
I have already lived.
What will the coming days &
weeks & years be like?
     I wonder...
     I wonder still...

reflections...

September 28

Holistic medicine, it is called- the recognition that mind & body are fully intertwined, that what we think and believe and feel affects, is lived out in our physical body. And perhaps we don't like to believe that because it puts far more responsibility for our health and well-being in our own hands than we would like to accept. Yet I believe deeply in the wisdom, the knowledge of our bodies.

more body language

In every disease there is a message...
the body trying to tell us something
   about ourselves
   about our life
the symptoms clues to what is
out of balance- if we will only
listen, pay attention.

But the great modern
commandment of sickness is
     GET WELL!
And so we try to eradicate our
symptoms before hearing their
messages...wipe them out before
listening to the truths they
long to tell...treating the symptoms
rather than facing their source.

Illness is often the body's call
for change- in priority or posture
    attitude or approach
and healing, whether we like
this truth or not, is often the
by-product of that change.

Perhaps good health is
largely the result of listening
to the things our body
tells us- and illness is the
reminder of what we have
forgotten.

248.

September 29

*We are messengers that have
forgotten our message.*
-A.J. Heschel

my message to the world...
Let go of fear!
Why should we fear
each other? Inside,
beneath the skin, we are
all the same...
yet we are individually
unique. It is a mystery,
a glorious mystery! So why
not spend our time & effort
in contemplating & unraveling
the wondrous mystery of
our simultaneous oneness &
uniqueness rather than
fighting over it? Why not
celebrate the wonder of
similarity & diversity as
two sides of the human coin?

If we can accept the gift
of *our own* uniqueness,
then we can honor the
uniqueness of every other
being- and his gifts, her
glory will not threaten
us but will create a
more beautiful, colorful
world...a world where
love & acceptance prevail...
a world transformed from
fear to love.
        Namaste.
        Shalom.
        Salaam.
        Let it be so.

September 30

God's love is received,
not achieved.
-Ted Loder

loving God...

What does it mean to
　love God?
Is it to love life?
Is it to love creation?
Is it to love others?
After all, if God is all in all,
　　　　if God is source & substance,
　　　　if God is creator & sustainer,
　　　　　then- ALL of the above...
　but perhaps even more,
　　it is to know
　　　you are LOVED
　　　　VALUED
　　　　ACCEPTED
　　　　CHERISHED...
and perhaps *that* is why it
　is such a challenge...
　　　　I wonder...

reflections...

OCTOBER ~
falling leaves

October 1

october

Cooler, darker mornings...
sunlight filtered now
through boughs of ever-changing
color...mums & asters nod
their heads of gold & mauve,
rust & crimson, as summer's
flowers fall on bended knee,
their strength & beauty
 nearly spent.

The garden's bounty
changes, too, as succulent
tomatoes give way to squash &
cabbage, pumpkin &
rutabaga, while the heady
fragrance of fresh apples
becoming applesauce fills
 the kitchen air.

The sun daily bids
an earlier good-by,
and occasionally overhead
come calls of goose
formations heading south.
Butterflies are gone, it seems,
and buzzing bees...falling
leaves dot the lawn and
earth's own pace begins
to slow as, all around,
nature begins to prepare
for winter's rest & restoration.

 It is blessed autumn.

252.

October 2

*I am a twenty-four-year survivor of breast cancer and this was written on the anniversary of my surgery which happened in 1984. I walk with the confidence that I am a person who **had** cancer...*

survival

from whence did it come,
this thing growing inside
my breast?
>   alien...
>   foreign...
>   fearsome...
>   the enemy...

yet here it is,
within this very body
I call home...
making itself 'at home',
>   a threat to my tranquility
>   my hope
>   my very life!

first come the tears,
>   the disbelief...
>   the sense of helplessness & grief...

but nipping at their heels comes
anger, accompanied by fierce determination-
>   "Out, out damned spot!
>   damned misplaced growth!
>   You are not welcome here!
>   Whatever hospitality you found
>   within my body, spirit, mind
>   which issued invitation is
>   now withdrawn!
>   My goal is LIFE!
>   wholeness!
>   healing!
>   and I *will* survive!
>   Alive!"

We're given second chances every day of our life.
We don't usually take them, but they're there for the taking.
-Andrew M. Greeley

253.

October 3

*...to continue this crazy thing called writing might lead to
steep precipices, dangerous canyons, craggy cliffs.*
-Natalie Goldberg

what do you know?

"Write what you know,"
the experts say, so...
   I know how to bandage wounds...
         how to give CPR...
         how to bake a pie & mouth-watering cookies...
         how to drive...
         how to play the piano.
   I know how to read
         how to add & subtract, multiply & divide.
   I know how to change a diaper...
         how to quiet a fussy baby.
   I know how to walk & talk & sing...
         how to use a screwdriver...
         how to send an e-mail.
    but all of these are "how-tos"...
So what do I *know?*
   that life is precious but finite.
   that pain does not kill.
   that grief must be expressed in order to end.
   that the world will go on without me.
   that my children are not mine but belong to
       themselves and the world.
   that the spiritual journey never ends.
   that love is an ephemeral & tenuous &
       precious thing.
   that coffee & chocolate are essential foods.
   that the best 'healthy' foods are tomatoes
       & peaches & corn-on-the-cob
   that hope does indeed spring eternal.
   that we cannot heal other people.
   that a thread of connection links all creation
           and
   that it is possible to live with a broken heart...
       but who wants to read about that?

254.

October 4

There is one world only,
the one to which we give ourselves
utterly, and to which one day
we are blessed to return.
-David Whyte

a psalm of confusion

Thoughts tumble over
one another...an almost
overwhelming cacophony
of voices from the soul's
depth, crying out to
    be heard.
And over- or under- them all
is the quiet voice of despair
which whispers, 'Not enough time...
    not enough time.'
The mature adult part of
my self knows that *all* learning,
all wisdom does not have to be,
cannot be accomplished in
    this lifetime.
But the child in me wants it
ALL- here...now!
O Spirit, help me not to let
the time I have slip through
my fingers. Let me make
it count in some way. Permit
me to leave an *imprint* of
my life for those who follow,
a sign that I have walked
    this way.
Grant me a glimpse, if you
will, of immortality. Let my
life make a difference...
an impact...an impression.
Open me to the holy paradox
of living life fully and letting go.
And bless me and every beloved one
with your presence & peace this day.
    Let it be so.

October 5

That is sanctity: the wholeness of giving the gift of all your self.
Not waiting till that self is fine and moral and healthy and
balanced enough to expose. -**Rowan Williams**

stripping down...
Over the years,
I have ejected lots
of spiritual "baggage:
which no longer
served me well.

I am trying to
"travel light"...to
shed the constraints
of tenets, creeds,
beliefs which only
bind, which no
longer fit.

Is there some
blessedness, I
wonder, in walking
around
        naked?

October 6

seeing...
What do I see as
I go through my day?
Do I see- *really* see-
the beauty and richness
and comfort of my home?
The deep blue walls of the
living room...the cheery yellow
in the dining room...the lovely
wood floors and high ceilings
and wide white woodwork and
the screened front porch...
so much a part of my daily life

that I frequently take them for
granted, losing the deep appreciation
such loveliness should engender.

 Do I see- *and appreciate-*
the refrigerator and stove,
the washer and dryer, the
mixer and blender and toaster
which make preparing meals
a pleasure, rather than
a labor-intensive chore?
and the food filling pantry and
refrigerator shelves- more than
sufficient to feed & sustain-
do I truly *see* & give thanks?

Do I see- and give thanks
for- my dependable car which
takes me where I need &
want to go?

Do I see- really see- the faces
& lives of all I encounter,
treating them with respect and
honoring them as God's own
created & beloved children?

O Light of Lights,
    Source of Truth,
    Show-er of the Way,
        open my eyes this day.
        Open my heart to behold
        the everyday, ordinary,
        extraordinary gifts that
        populate my life.
        Create in me a renewed,
        thankful, loving heart.
        Be my vision- let me live with
            eyes wide open
            arms wide open
            heart wide open.
                    Amen & amen   257.

October 7

Sunday

I have felt bereft lately-
so very far away from God,
whose face seems perpetually
hidden...whose loving grace
seems withheld from me- or
at least from my awareness,
my ability to grasp it...
   and so, I will go to
   church today, become
   part- for a short while- of
   a communion of saints,
   a community of sinners,
   uniting my heart & mind &
   voice with others who come
   seeking for God...
      and perhaps, in the midst
      of the music & prayers,
      of sharing the peace &
      receiving the bread & wine,
      I will see the face of God.

October 8

*There are only two great fears that should exist in a person's life,
the fear of deceiving oneself and the fear of imitating someone else.*
-Marc Gafni

today's truth

I WAS BORN WHERE I WAS BORN.
I WAS GIVEN THE GIFTS I WAS GIVEN.
I WAS GRANTED THE OPPORTUNITIES
   THAT ARE MINE.
MY GOAL IN THE WORLD IS TO BE
   THE BEST ME THAT I CAN BE.
I HAVE NO DESIRE TO BE ANYONE
   OTHER THAN MYSELF.

258.

October 9

Words are power...the world can change on a word.
-Christina Baldwin

reading joy

When did the squiggles on the page,
spoken into life by Pop-pop, Mom, &
John begin to speak to me?
      to become words instead
         of only lines & shapes?

What connections in my brain-
or magic in my soul- brought the
language into being,
      causing me to read for myself?

How did the spoken word
become transformed, prestidigitated,
into something so magical,
      mysterious, ordinary,
        that I could discern it for myself?

I only remember the joy,
the total satisfaction,
the incredible excitement of
      knowing how to read!

October 10

morning reflections

How short the days are getting.
Through the thinning leaves
of my dear Japanese maple,
the street light still shines
and though crickets serenade,
no birdsong yet caresses
the morning air. The candle
flickering at my side reflects
in the window, darkened still,
while sounds of human life
seem far away-

the swish of cars not yet
giving way to daytime traffic's
roar. Deep peace...
it settles in & 'round
me, blanketing my
heart & soul with
God's own loving Presence...
an awareness that I
have again been
gifted with another
day of life...the hours
ahead spread out like
a golden path which I
can walk as I choose,
always aware that *how*
I walk and *what* I choose
will affect you- and you-
and every you who at
this moment draws a breath
in dawn's ebbing darkness or
in the velvet black of night.

O Indwelling, Enlivening
Spirit, guide me to
compassionate choices this
day...to steps of integrity &
intentionality...an awareness
that all I do & all I say touches
the rest of the world- like the
beating of butterfly wings in
Brazil...bearing the gift of good
or ill...blessing or curse.
The choice is mine.
Amen & amen
Let it be so.

The world is round and the place which may seem like the end may also be the beginning. -Ivy Baker Priest

260.

October 11

foreign landscapes

When the landscape of your
   world becomes foreign, unfamiliar
when the path ahead is unclear &
   even threatening
when all familiar landmarks
   vanish and you are walking
   the rocky terrain of the
   heart...
      THIS is the time for self-care:
         sleep- long & deep...
         nourishing food...
         fun...
         re-creation...
         caring as gently for
         yourself as for a wounded
            friend.
And as you hold yourself gently,
cherish yourself deeply, you'll
find yourself once again on the
familiar path that leads
              to home.

October 12

'It is more blessed to give than to receive.'- so goes the old adage. But isn't it also a 'gift' to receive what is offered to us by another? To graciously open hands and heart when another person presents us with a part of his joy, a part of her pain?

giving

We talk so much about giving-
and it is indeed a blessed thing
to do- to give our gifts, our talents,
time, to help another...
      to a good cause...
     to share our bounty
        and our selves.

But isn't it also a gift,
I wonder, to be open
to *receive*- another's
thoughts, another's pain,
another's truth,
another's *gift?*
O P E N
O　P　E　N
O　　P　　E　　N
Open heart
open ears
open eyes
open mind
open life.
     Isn't this also a precious gift
     we can give to another?
     Receiving what they have
          to give?

*If we've ever been on the receiving end of an act of mercy that made
a difference in our lives, we have seen the face of God.*
-Kathleen Norris

October 13

seeing...again

The man born blind asked
Jesus for healing...to *see*
the world around him. And so,
Jesus responded- only to have
the man see without clarity
     that first time.
Perhaps it was just too much
to take in- this world and all
     that's in it-
perhaps it overwhelmed
the man with more than
he could handle- both beauty & ugliness
         joy & pain
         welcome & exclusion-

and his mind shouted,
"Stop! Enough! Wait!"
to give his heart a chance
to catch up.
Then Jesus spoke again, and laid
on hands, and clarity & light flooded
heart & mind & eye and the man
SAW the world as it was, as it IS-
the total picture, fully fleshed out...
and though at that
moment he rejoiced,
surely there were days
to come when he would
wonder if this seeing were
blessing or curse...

October 14

inner wisdom

You have an inner
source of wisdom.
Call it what you
will: intuition
the voice of God
spiritual guidance
beginner's mind
inner knowing
To find the source, to tap into the living
water that flows
from it, to be filled,
you have to be
willing to go deeply...
to open fully...
to risk completely...
and then-
to receive totally.
The gift is yours-
do you dare
to receive it?

October 15

Each life is clothed in raiment of spirit that secretly links it to everythings else. -John O'Donohue

clothed

'The spiritual clothing one
person wears can never fit
the soul of another.'- so say
the ancient Celts. Yet we modern
folk insist the garb of spirituality
be 'one-size-fits-all'...losing in this
homogeneity the awareness of the
    beauty and uniqueness
    of individuality.
Some days, I wear the
cheerful garb of rainbow
colors, of swirling patterns,
of rustling, swaying fabrics
    which enhance & enliven
    my dancing walk...
On others, I reach for somber
gray & black, the muted blue
of denim, fabrics both quiet
and still, accompanying my
    silent way through
    thoughtfulness &
    remembered grief.
And much as I would like to
shed my garb at times to
clothe myself in yours, I know
it will not fit...and you cannot
wear mine...
    the best we can do, I think,
    is walk together, hand in hand,
    in loving company and holy
    admiration for the way in
    which our clothing fits,
    enhances, beautifies,
    defines who we each are.

264.

October 16

My dad was a big, boisterous, loud-talking, warm-hearted man. He also possessed more integrity, more innate honesty, than any other person I have ever known. Over the years of my growing up, he and I clashed often- he always thought he was right- but some of my happiest childhood memories contain times spent with him and I miss him to this very day.

birthday memories

Dad's birthday- he would
have been eighty-nine today.
Wherever you are, dad,
I love you.
    For so many years, I
    heard Mom's voice coming
    from my mouth...saw Mom's
    face in my mirror...
        but I am becoming
        more & more aware of those parts
        of me that are like *you*...
            realizing I *am* "my father's
                            daughter"...
Our best times were my
college years, when you
would take me out to
dinner in New York City...and
we would *talk*...
    gratitude overflows
    for those days.

How we remember, what we remember, and why we remember form the most personal map of our individuality.
-Christina Baldwin

I'm so sorry you could
never really talk about
Carl's death- actually either one.
You held your grief inside,
never sharing your anguish over
your son-in-law and grandson...
    you- loquacious & out-going as
    you were- never found words
    to express your grief.
        And Rennie, too- Mom said
        you never talked about the
        death of your youngest
                        daughter.

You buried it all so deeply-
  perhaps that's what over-
  burdened your heart...

Well, now you're with all of them -
and I can hear your laughter,
  as words & joy flow freely
  in the corridors of heaven.
   I miss that laugh-
   but I'll hear it again one day.
    I love you, Dad.
      Happy birthday!

October 17

happiness

Two questions
rebound in the
space of head & heart...
echo in the deep
places of the soul...
  why be unhappy
  about something
  you *can* change?
   AND
  why be unhappy
  about something
  you *cannot* change?

A challenge...
a two-pronged koan...
a scalpel plunging
 deeply to the heart
 of the matter,
 to find and free the
   truth-
    if I am willing
    to pay attention.

266.

October 18

freedom

Am I willing to take
the risks of freedom- to define
"discipleship" and "leadership"
for myself, rather than conforming
to the ideas & opinions
    of others?
Do I fear seeing what others
do *not* see? Yes & no...
    yes, because I fear being misunderstood,
      being seen as "peculiar" or "crazy"...
    no, because what I see is *real*...what
      I know is *truth*...what I experience
      is an unfolding, ongoing journey-
        and I would not go back
        to where I was!
Of course the steps are often
fearsome...looking back over
my shoulder can bring longing
for other times & places...
    but always the Holy Presence
                pulls...
                tugs...
                pushes...
                prods...
                leads.
Being in step with
the Divine can mean-
often *does* mean- being
    out-of-step with everyone else...
      not in arrogance but
      in all humility...
        allowing others to be
        where *they* are as I am
            where *I* am...

267.

October 19

Grant us, O God, your protection, and in your protection, strength;
and in strength, understanding; and in understanding, knowledge;
and in knowledge, the knowledge of justice; and in the knowledge of justice,
the love of justice; and in that love, the love of existence;
and in the love of existence, the love of God, God and all goodness.
-Ancient Welsh prayer

from the heart

Heart of my heart-
this is what you are,
    brother Christ...
the heart of my heart.
And I find myself
drawn to you...
    to your way
    to your path
    to your guidance
Often, I am a poor traveler...
my wayfaring far from the
path you seem to have made-
but I find my deepest learnings
come when I *stray* from the
beaten path...
    and perhaps it is
    not straying at all
    but rather- with fear &
    trepidation- stepping
    out in faith to where
I hear your voice calling to me...
    to see the burning bush
    to hear the singing bird
    to touch the hurting friend
    to write the words of
        my innermost thoughts
    to laugh & cry & feel
        deeply
    to be all I have been
        created to be.

268.

October 20

Writing is language made tangible. experience saved and savored, life transformed into story. -Christina Baldwin

on writing...
Do I write so I
can leave a piece
of myself behind?
So I will not just
fade away and
be lost?
      That old, old fear...
         of BEING no more...
The reality is,
death *will* take place-
and whatever happens to
the life force is out of
my control-
      but I can write my life...
             my thoughts...
             my hopes...
             my dreams...
     for my children & grandchildren...
        even if no one else
        ever reads a word
     I can say, "This is who I am..."
and who I have been
and how I came to be
      that person.
Breathe on me, Creator...Spirit...
     breathe into me.
Give me a voice...
       words...
       courage to speak.
     This is my prayer,
        my wish.
        my dream,
        my intent.
            LET IT BE SO.

October 21

To recognize evil and not to oppose it is to surrender your humanity;
to recognize evil and to oppose it with the waepons of the evil-doer
is to enter into your humanity; to recognize evil and to oppose it
with the weapons of God is to enter into your divinity.
-Mahamta Gandhi

responsibility

Being responsible takes
work. How much easier
to live without regard for
how what I do- and do *not-*
affects this planet and its
           living things.
Recycling...composting...using
a rain barrel...changing to low
energy light bulbs...lowering
the thermostat in winter,
raising it in summer...short
showers...less laundry...the list
is long, and I am proud of my
efforts- and yet-
           when I look at the faces
           of my grandchildren,
           of *any* children, I
           wonder- am I doing
           enough to secure their
           future? To insure that
           this Great Blue Planet
           will sustain their lives...
           their children's lives?
And so I seek to be
informed...to contact my
senators & congressman...
to live wisely & well & responsibly
each and every day...
           but being responsible
           takes work- and sometimes,
                      I am very tired.
           (Thank God it's not ALL up to me!)

270.

October 22

*We can't run from who we are, with our short tempers, our vanity,
our sharp tongues, our talents for self-aggrandizement, self-delusion,
or despair. But we can convert, in its root meaning of turn around,
so that we are forced to face ourselves as we really are. We can pray
that God will take our faults and use them for the good.*
-Kathleen Norris

inner work

Within each one of us
is something that wants
to keep things as they are...
   and it is both strange &
   frightening to discover
   that what binds us is
      what gives us comfort...
      makes us feel safe...

Within each one of us
are hardened, self-defeating patterns
we would rather not face...
and so we externalize
them and name them
"enemy"...
   and it is both strange &
   frightening to discover
   that which we fear & fight &
      hate is really within ourselves...

Within each one of us
are short-comings, those
"less-than" selves we
need to acknowledge, confess...
   and it is both strange &
   frightening to discover
   that the only way to
   change is to acknowledge
   who & how we *are*...
      and to know, with certainty.
      that our inner work
         is never done.

October 23

Life is not hurrying
on to a receding future nor hankering after
an imagined past. It is the turning
aside like Moses to the miracle
of the lit bush. To a brightness
that seems as transitory as your youth
once, but is the eternity that awaits you.
              -R.S. Thomas

deep yearning

I am yearning...
    but the focus is vague.
        I think it is for love...for arms to hold,
                    a body to touch,
                    lips to kiss,
                    ears to listen.
I yearn for contact...
        the ET touch of connection...
        the Michelangelo touch of God...
            but in human flesh.
"We crash so we can touch each other,"
said the detective in the movie
of that name. Is that all we know now,
        after all these centuries of existence?
            Why can't we go deep?
                    be genuine?
I WANT TO BE GENUINE...
        through & through...
        truly & fully myself.
            Light & dark, good & bad,
            in toto...born anew each day,
            resurrected from the garbage heaps
            of existence.
What I am seeking, I believe,
on this life journey is
to be born anew, over & over & over again...
    and the Church calls this redemption
                    salvation.
        I call it truly BEING myself.

272.

October 24

Being truthful about where I am spiritually, about where I have arrived at this point in my journey, is a risky thing. And I don't know if I am bring brave or foolish to include this writing, but here's to honesty and new life!

jesus talk

Certain kinds of "Jesus talk"
make me uncomfortable.
There- I said it, perhaps
risking life & limb in some circles.
But to say that one escaped injury
in a traffic accident because
"Jesus was there and took care
of me", (as I heard a perfectly nice
woman say recently) makes
my teeth hurt!
What about those who die
each day, in traffic accidents
or from illness- or in the throes
of war? Does this mean Jesus
does not care about *them?* that
their families did not pray hard
enough? Or is it indicative of
the state of their faith- or lack of it?
  And how exclusivist
  and judgmental is *that?*

"Jesus died for my sins" (words
from which, I confess, I usually
shrink) means, to me, that Jesus
was the one who showed me my
dark side, my deepest humanness,
my self-absorption; the one who
held & holds a mirror before me
to make me aware of my
deep needs; the one who has blazed
the trail of transformation, which
can occur only through awareness
and forgiveness of self & others...
LETTING GO of what
keeps us bound.

More difficult words: "Jesus rose from
the dead." I have come to believe that
the resurrection was & is a
metaphor for this deep and total
transformation; the dying to self...
the letting go of what has been
in order that there may be
something new, reshaped, reborn;
a new self- yet still recognizable
as self, but able to accomplish
so much more.

This kind of "Jesus talk" I understand.
And in this sense for me,
        Jesus LIVES.
        Jesus is Lord...
            the primary moving force
            behind, in & through my life.
            Amen & amen

*If we are unwilling to live askew for a while, to be set off balance,
to wait on the ever spacious threshold, we remain in the same old room
for all our lives.* **-Richard Rohr**

reflections...

October 25

facing change...

WAIT!   In the midst of change,
         in the wildernesses of life-
WAIT!   for God's guidance...
         for the word of the Spirit...
         for healing to happen...
WAIT!   reaching out for help & support...
         praying for patience & guidance...
WAIT!   like Elijah in the desert...
         here in your own wilderness...
         in the midst of chaos...
WAIT!   Treat yourself gently...
         Be good to yourself...
         Don't demand too much
                 of yourself...
WAIT!   And it *will* come to pass.

October 26

morning

Overcast morning- but
no sense of gloom casts
over my heart
Only the sense of peace,
of quiet without & within
Gentle sounds surround
and fill me- birdsong
        a breeze through the trees
        the lilt of music
        the whisper of the fan
        the quiet exhale of my own breath
Gracious One Who Creates,
grant me the gift
   of continuing peace this day
   of hope to uplift my spirit
   of gratitude for the
      holiness of life

of laughter to lighten any
    load I carry
of compassion for each one
    to cross my path
of joy & a sense of completion
        when this day ends.

...moments that should each last forever
Slide unconsciously by us like water.
-Kenneth Rexroth

October 27

mice sing!

Mice sing to each other!
So I learned from NPR
yesterday...
mice *sing*- in voices only
other mice can hear.
Mice SING!
Isn't that a lovely image?
In spite of their
dreadful gnawing
habits, in spite of their
image as annoying pests,
they SING!
    and how will I now ever
    be able to set another
    mousetrap in my
    basement- as I picture
    Gus-Gus, Jacques & friends
    serenading this Cinderella?

276.

October 28

I have some of the most amazingly beautiful friends, many of them women in their fifties, sixties, and seventies. Their beauty has been achieved without cosmetic surgery, either reducing or 'enhancing' body parts, but simply by the experience of LIVING. It saddens me that our culture, our society, fails to recognize and acknowledge the incredible beauty of the aging woman, the full-blown rose releasing her fragance to an often-oblivious world.

menopause

A time of shapeshifting-
so says author Alice Walker...
    and I love this image!
For indeed, my shape
has shifted, and my face,
   and my way of thinking.
A glorious gift in so many
ways, when the creativity
inherent in the womb shifts
to other places, finds expression
in other ways, the ending of
one gift giving way to so
many others.
So why do we continue
to see bodily 'perfection'
spelled Y-O-U-T-H,
instead of glorying in
the mature beauty and
fulfillment of age?

A crone is a woman who has wisdom, compassion,
humor, courage, and vitality.
-Jean Shinoda Bolen

reflections...

October 29

*You only grow by coming to the end of something and
by beginning something else.*
-John Irving

anticipation...
'What do you want?' Lyn asked.
'What would you WANT to do-
   if you had your choice?'
Easy- I would go to Iona
for a month...
   to walk, think, write,
   to absorb the holy energy
   there. Yes, yes, YES!
More than anything else,
that is what I want.

Life doesn't permit it at
present, but naming it makes
it something to look forward to,
                  to save for,
                  to anticipate,
                  to prepare for-
not at the expense of the present,
but to have as a dream before me...
                  a soft focus...
                  an eye-squint of
                  a time in the distance,
                  coming ever closer, but
                  at an indefinable pace.

And in the meanwhile,
a nearer, clearer focus-
   on making each day holy...
   on recognizing & acknowledging
      the gifts & blessings...
   on permitting today's cares &
      problems to flow through me
      like the ocean tides...
   on involving myself in the state
      of the state...
      in this fall's election.

God, grant me serenity...inner peace...
   hope...compassion.
Empower me to let go of anger...
   frustration...judgment.
Grant that I may use my financial
   resources wisely & well...
   that I may simplify my life &
   possessions.
Empower me to care
   wisely & well for my body,
   to value & cherish & honor it.
Help me to be deeply & truly present
   in the moments of my life
   and grant me hope & patience &
   holy compassion.
         Let it be so.

October 30

It is strange to be here. The mystery never leaves you alone.
-John O'Donohue

writing poetry

More about finding
than choosing...
about alertness...
stepping back
and letting go...
about finding,
arriving at...
all the while working at...
with repeated and intimate
attention to the materials
at hand-
pen, paper, words, images...
the unexplainable
convergence of ideas...
the awareness of connections.
and most of all,
   about mystery...

October 31

all hallows eve

Three flocks of geese heading
south...rapidly-falling leaves...
autumn is quickly passing.
Rock me gently, Spirit.
Let my heart & life continue
to heal, in this autumn of
my life.
Let me touch the truth of
who I am-
     and LIVE it.

Breathe into me deep peace
                    compassion
                    wisdom.

Blessings today on all I love...
                    on all who need healing...
                    on all whose spirits
                    remain unsettled...
                    on this 'house' in which I live,
                              this body.
                    Amen & amen

reflections...

NOVEMBER -
the days grow short

November 1 - the Celtic New Year

As I reviewed the poems and prayers written during and for the month of November, as the darkness lengthens and the light seems to move further & further away, I realized that they focus on birth and death: birth, new life, expressed in creativity, in my writing; death expressed in losses, and in my grieving.

"and it came to pass..."

The phone broke into
the after-midnight silence...
the message which
came shattering my life into
a million pieces, never to be
gathered together in the same
way again.

> How does the mind
> grasp the immensity
> of the death of a
> child? *your* child?

It is the thinnest time of the year, the season at which the veil between time and eternity can easily become transparent, the time when darkness overtakes the light.
-Esther De Waal

A sense of unreality
hovered over the next hours,
the next days...in the
midst of people trying to
help, of others sharing
my grief, I was dreadfully alone,
and the only words
I could offer to the
One who had always been
my strength, my firm rock,
were, "Oh, God...oh, God...oh, God,"
unsure of what I
meant, if blessing or curse;
uncertain of what I wanted-
except to have
my child back!

Time passed in a blur...days uniformly
gray, shapeless, without meaning. I
sleep-walked through life, deceiving
those around me into believing
I was *fine...*

while deep inside I
was bleeding out from
the wound only I
could feel...

Weeping drained my life-force,
leaving me a shapeless husk,
a gaunt, gray form in the
mirror, unrecognizable
        even to me.
Calendar days ceased to
have meaning, as Grief
extracted a toll which
Age had not, imprinting
herself in countless ways
upon my countenance...
    tear-traced furrows
    lining my face...the heavy
    burden of loss bending
    my back...

And it came to pass,
one day- a lifetime later in
the non-linear scheme of
things eternal-
one day I awoke
and put on a red
dress- and laughed!
            It's called survival-
                    and grace.

November 2

writing
It is in the connections
that the writer finds her hope;
it is for the chance encounter
that she feels called to share
her story, always hoping that
her words will resonate with
another heart, that a resounding

"Yes" will issue from the one
touched by the shared truth.
The struggle is a mighty one.
It takes courage, dedication,
discipline. For me, it is
an on-going wrestling match
with my fears, my sense of
inadequacy, my shaky certainty
that it has all been said
before- and better.

But here I sit- coffee at my side,
pen in hand, Mozart on the CD
player, the clock ticking the
seconds gently away. Being
present in this moment means
putting thoughts on paper-
nothing less, nothing more.

I find I live in this
place of needing to *tell...*
needing to weigh & examine,
to assess & explain how
I experience the world-
for whom I do not know.
Perhaps only for myself-
an audience of one, plodding
doggedly along this road
of life, uncertain of the
destination, certain only that
often, company is welcome;
but that ultimately, I walk
alone in the Divine Company-
   that oxymoronic, mysterious,
   experience of
   accompanied aloneness.
   And so I write.

We do not write in order to be understood, we write in order to understand.
-Cecil Day-Lewis

284.

November 3

Sitting in my chair in the early morning, breathing deeply with eyes closed and heart open, sometimes I hear the voice of God...not aloud, to be sure, but deep in the stillness of my heart, in the place where my intuition & creativity dwell.

wholly conversation

What do you want me
to do? I ask...
    LISTEN...only LISTEN,
    the Divine responds.
To what?
    To the leadings of your heart.
My heart? In what way?
    The way of creativity...
            of choice.
I'm confused...
    What is the deepest desire
    of your heart?
To write...to dance...to love
someone with my whole heart...
    So...what is stopping you?
Time...
    You have as much
    as anyone else.
Fear...
    You're getting warmer.
    What else?
You're God- surely you know!
    Oh, I do- but so do you.
I am deeply afraid of
letting go...
    because...
of being judged...of being
hurt...of being left.
    But I am always here.
Take my fear, please...
    But will you give it up?
Help me...help me. Amen

grief's labyrinth

My heart is filled with grief
this morning...weighs a ton...
   my mood matching
    the grayness of the day.
Open the well of my heart, O God...
   whoever you are,
   however you are.
Let me drink deeply of the water
   of life which bubbles there...
           refreshing...
           life-giving...
For deep within, I know there
is a place where Wisdom dwells-
   and joy and peace.
The path seems so direct-
and yet I find that as I journey,
there are twists & turns...
        unexpected dead ends...
I must retrace my steps...select
      another fork in the road.
And as I can see the center
of the labyrinth from every point,
but can reach it only by
negotiating every twist and turn
in the path, so goes my life...
   though sometimes the way to
   my center is clouded & obscure-
   and I am not at all sure
   I am on the right road or
   headed in the right direction.
Grief is like that...a gray fog...
   a shroud which envelops me,
    clouding my vision,
    obscuring the road ahead,
      until every choice seems impossible...
      life reaches an impasse-
   and I stand transfixed,
   unable to move either forward or back,

frozen deep in grief's foggy grasp...
eyes clouded with tears
                              yet again.
I need the sun to shine!
Even the candle at my elbow offers
little light or warmth or courage.
   The clock ticks relentlessly...
   and inside, a cold wind blows.
   I am chilled to the bone.
      Will it never end?
      Will I ever be warm again?
Open your arms to hold me,
O God...cradle, comfort, warm me,
      lest my frozen heart stops beating.

Bad times have a scientific value...
We learn geology the morning after the earthquake.
-Ralph Waldo Emerson

November 5

transformation
To live in rhythm with
The flow of seasons,
The flow of what the body needs,
Requires reflection...
And reverence for
The gifts of Mother Nature,
Mother Earth.

There is a time of fullness & abundance
And a time of seeking refuge...
Of fallowness & rest
To permit healing & renewal...
A time when restoration happens...
And when the realization comes,
Like the dawning of a new day,
That you are whole and
Filled with creativity
Once more.

287.

November 6

'We are each a multiple personality that has learned to act in concert.'-words that are rattling around in my brain, but whether they express an original idea or are something I have absorbed, I do not know. And isn't that often the way of things?

bits & pieces

Do we ever *really* know another person?
Each of us has so many faces, so many
selves, in & through whom we live...
as if, in any given moment
     in any given encounter
   some inner "secretary" shuffles
   through our personal Rolodex,
   selecting the appropriate
   persona for there & then.
Oh, we can, we *do* deny that we are
doing this...we can claim authenticity
for ourselves...but how much of our
   deepest selves do we really
   share? How much do *I* share?-
        for this is very personal.
The people in my life each know pieces
of me, facets of this complexity that
I am...as I put on my various faces,
   selecting the one that seems right
   for the situation.
I *learned* to do this...
we learned to do this...
   though I am not
   sure exactly how...
how we have gone from being open,
spontaneous, trusting children to
being often-guarded, closed adults
who allow only pieces of ourselves-
our truest selves- to slip out...
tantalizing hints of who we might be-
   if we/I ever let go.

November 7

I do not understand my own actions. For I do not do what I want,
but I do the very thing I abhor. Romans 7:15

stripped clean

The things I know that
I *should* do to care for
body, mind & soul,
                    I DO NOT DO...
the things I know that
I should *not* do because
they harm my body, sap
my strength, drain my
spirit,
                    I DO!

The words are so familiar...
they resonate across the
ages, slip from the pages
of my bible to lie in my
lap...
        unkempt, slimy things of
        which I want no part-
                    yet there they are,
                    like maggots feeding on
                    the rotting flesh of all
                    my good intentions...
                    they will not leave until
                    I am stripped clean,
                    down to the bone,
                            to the place of truth & honesty.

Only then can I stand before
my God and say,
        "Can we begin again today?"

November 8

It is a day bright with sunshine. Then, from somewhere, unexpected, comes a veil of mist and then another, until the face of the sun is hid from us, and all is dark before our eyes. Yet we never doubt for a moment the sun is still there.
-Helen Keller

silent prayer

The man we have come to know
as Saint Paul conveyed to the
church at Rome- and so to us-
one of his greatest pieces of wisdom
when he wrote:
>"The Spirit helps up in our weakness;
>for we do not know how to pray as
>we ought, but that very Spirit intercedes
>for us with sighs *too deep for words.*"

Sometimes- or so it seems to me-
the very best prayer, the deepest,
truest prayer, is SILENCE...
>emptying oneself of the noise
>of daily living & coming to a place
>of complete awareness,
>>where words fail but
>>where connection exists fully.

In times of deepest emotion,
>words do fail us; we simply FEEL...
>>the overwhelming joy,
>>the heart-rending grief...
>and putting it all into words is
>beyond our ability,
>beyond our desire.

Instead, the Spirit of the
Living God that dwells within us,
enlivens us, *breathes* for us
>"with sighs too deep for words."

I love that image...
and it became my lifeline
following the sudden death of
>my eldest son,

when the abyss of my grief threatened
to swallow me alive...when the only
cry of my broken heart was, "My
God, my God, my God..."
unsure of whether this
was curse or prayer...
certain only that I HAD NO WORDS
for either the Divine or
human presences in my life.

Pain became my home-
and in that dark, lonely place
I lived, uncertain if I were
alive or dead, knowing only
that *I could not pray.*
After all, what would I ask?
To have my son restored to life,
like Lazarus?
To turn back the clock so that
I could persuade him not to
make that fateful trip to Mexico?
To have my life be over- when
I still had three children who
loved and needed me?

What? How? there were no words.
But the love of friends & family
surrounded me...
the breath, the sighs of the Spirit
prayed *for* me...
the sun continued to rise
each day...
and slowly,
slowly,
slowly
I began to heal...
and pray.

November 8

...if we are all vessels of the divine, how can we use religion to justify destruction of other human beings?
-Joan Chittister

Election Day

How can a person be 'pro-life'
    and also be pro-war?
    support the death penalty
    while opposing abortion?
If a life is a life is a life,
    what gives one life more
    value than another?
And if all life has value,
    why does humanity's place
    take precedence over all
    other living creatures on
    this planet?
I struggle with this
seemingly oxymoronic
worldview which seems
to proliferate exponentially
in each election year...
    and wonder about
    easy answers,
    facile solutions,
    and the politics of appeasement...
        as I wait in line to
        cast my ballot.

November 10

signs along the way

I saw a sign the other day-
    PRAY THE HARDEST
    WHEN IT'S HARDEST TO PRAY
And just how does one do that?
      I believe in the power
      of prayer- though I have
      no idea of how it "works".

I believe that when I pray,
I open myself to the collective energy
of good & God in this world.
When I pray deeply, from the
truest part of myself, I am opening
myself to being changed, enlightened...
　　asking that my eyes & mind & heart
　　be opened to new possibilities.
　　　　And it is *not* about changing
　　　　　　God's mind or heart, but mine,
　　　　　　　　and the world's.

When I pray for peace,
I know that peace must begin
within me; that when I am in
turmoil, I send out into the
world a sense of disquiet.
When I live in fear, I add my fear
to the fears of the world.
When I live in anger, I add my
small piece of anger to the anger already
rampant on this beleaguered planet.
　　　　But flapping my butterfly wings
　　　　of peace & love & trust here in
　　　　High Point, North Carolina, United States
　　　　of America, Western hemisphere, planet
　　　　Earth, Milky Way galaxy,
　　　　　　WILL and DOES effect what is
　　　　　　happening in Iraq, in North Korea,
　　　　　　　　in Burma, in Pakistan, in Sudan,
　　　　　　　　in Tibet, in Washington, D.C.
　　　　　　　　　　Let it be so.

reflections...

November 11

This is the excitement that fuels the writing life:
the desire for what might emerge when the imagination
begins to travel the crowded seas of the white page.
-John O'Donohue

still writing...

Writing begins from
a place of not knowing...
it involves taking risks...
   diving into the unknown...
    to deep, new, old places inside yourself.
It may lead to steep precipices,
dangerous canyons,
craggy cliffs...
  but always, it is
  an adventure,
  a journey into the
    mysterious, beautiful,
    stunning magic that is life.

Writing means following the path
before you...picking up a pen and
facing the terrifying whiteness
  of the empty page...
    and then- JUST DOING IT,
      enjoying the tears &
      laughter along the way.

November 12

It is my joy; it is my challenge; it is my nemesis; it is my call; it is often my
raison d'etre: writing.

more writing

I have been wrestling with my
Muse, the Wise Woman who
dwells deep inside my heart & mind,
the Breath of God which enlivens
the force of creativity...hanging on
for dear life as I try to extract a
blessing...

"I will not let go until I receive
the blessing of my own voice,"
              I vow breathlessly...
"until I have your
promise of co-creation."
"Then pick up your pen," comes
the Voice...
       and the wind of the Spirit blows in &
       through & around me
                   as I begin
                   to write.

November 13

Every word is born in silence and returns to silence.
-Ambrose Wathen

falling leaves
"Ave Maria" fills the air inside,
    an accompaniment
    to the ballet of falling
    leaves outside my window.
I have never before simply
watched leaves fall...
    never realized the infinite
    variety of their paths
    from branch to earth...
          that one whirling in
              dizzying circles,
          another wending its
              way lazily in ever-widening
                  arcs...
          one falling straight down
              without impediment or delay,
          while another seeming to
              carom from branch to branch,
              tracing a difficult and
              long-delayed path.
          That one hangs up on a branch
              far above the ground, as
              if reluctant to take the
                  final plunge.

And now a breath of wind sets
a myriad into simultaneous
motion,
while right in front of me,
a yellow oak leaf spirals
its determined trajectory
earthward.
The music plays on-and I sit enchanted
by the spectacle in front of me.
The seasons changing before my eyes...
Nature shedding her autumn
gown to prepare for winter's
stark beauty.

November 14

the critic

In every writer's mind
there dwells a constant critic...
the commentator, editor,
pain-in-the-ass voice
that nay-says...
that makes you doubt
the validity of your own
thoughts, your own words,
your own voice.
And if you let it,
if you do not turn
the volume down, if
you do not confront
it face-to-face and
stare it down,
you will never
dare to write.

If my mind is crowded with ideas or thoughts or plans or other
people's creations there is less room for my own.
-Alice Walker

296.

November 15

*Open the window in the center of your chest,
and let the spirits fly in and out.*
-Rumi

connections

I saw the most amazing thing
today, as I was walking in the woods,
along the path beside the stream-
a yellow leaf dancing in mid-air-
   or so it seemed.
No connection could I see to
earth or tree, yet this small leaf
cavorted there, in celebration of its
   freedom, no longer held upon a branch
   but totally & completely   FREE...
      free to float across the path,
      sometimes near & sometimes
      further from my own delighted face.
I laughed aloud at this absurdity,
this seeming paradox of floating leaf
which did not fall, but stayed suspended
at the level of my wide-open eyes,
   enthralled as I was at
   her seeming delight.

And then, a puff of wind breathed
through the trees, and I was standing
in a shower of falling leaves, blown from
every direction, surrounding me with
their whispering descent-
   and my small leaf,
   released from the spider's filament
   which held her, relinquished
   her solo performance and
      joined the universal dance.

November 16

They ask me to remember
but they want me to remember
their memories
and I keep on remembering
mine.
                        –Lucille Clifton

the past

The past swirls around me...
I walk through the mists
seeing only dimly...yet occasionally
there is a clearing
and I glimpse the view
with startling clarity-
just a brief moment-
before the fog again
enshrouds me and I
find myself wondering
if it were real or imagined.

Memory is like that-
an occasional lifting of
the mind's misty curtain...
a moment of revelation-
and then darkness. And yet,
this sustains me somehow...
encourages me...lets me
know that I am real and
my life has meaning.

November 17

being a writer

It is a daring thing
to refer to oneself
as a writer...
        it takes courage to
        lay claim to
        that title...
But once we begin

to name ourselves
in this way, we begin to
pay attention as a "writer"...
    accumulating experiences
    and letting them ripen
    into the rich soil from
    which our art can bloom...
        mental composting...
seeing *everything*- every
experience- as an outward & visible
sign of an inward, invisible grace...
taking in, absorbing the
world around us...living with
      EYES WIDE OPEN!
acknowledging that what we *know*
matters less than
      how we tell it...
sifting through memories like soil
through a sieve, so that
the bright nuggets of truth
      come to light...
recognizing that instead of
owning our thoughts, we
let them come *through* us...
      sharing the deepest
      intimacies of our lives.
It is indeed a daring thing
to BE a writer...

> *Your own words are the*
> *bricks and mortar of*
> *the dreams you want to*
> *realize. Behind every word*
> *flows energy.*
> **-Sonia Choquette**

November 18

We gather the jugsaw pieces of our experience and
put them together in a story we tell and retell
until we get the memory right.
-Maureen Murdock

memory
What exactly is memory?
It is selective...it both distorts and
tries to make sense of the past.
Memory is a reflection-
of how we see ourselves...
of how we see others...
of how we see past events.
Perhaps it is purely invention...
simply life seen from a particular
point of view...an angle of perception.
And always, there are
GAPS- sometimes huge ones-
in what we recall.
Memory is a way of creating one's identity...
a way of making sense of
the relationship between
remembered images and
recalled feelings.
Memory is rarely whole or
factually correct...
we remember what
suits our needs & purposes...
what emerges through the
filters of time & experience & desire.
Memories-*what* we remember-
can never be separated
from our imagination...
but what is important about
memory is the meaning
we draw from it...
gathering the jigsaw pieces of
our experience and putting them
together until we get the
memory right.

300.

November 19

A self-imposed pilgrimage is a quest. -Joan Anderson

pilgrimage

A pilgrim is one
who makes a holy
journey...one who
often travels in good
company but, at the
deepest place, is solitary-
                in focus
                in experience
This pilgrimage
this spiritual journey
   has been
   continues to be
         the essence
         the heart
         the center
         the focus of my life.
Fellow pilgrim,
I welcome you to
walk with me...to share
the trials and joys of
         searching
         questioning
         doubting
         discovering
   always mindful that
   we will see with different eyes-
my experience will be *my*
experience and *yours* will be
yours, though in the sharing,
I may hear the resonance of
truth at a place where your
experience overlaps with,
touches mine, as-
     for that moment in time-
       we journey on a shared path.
       NAMASTE.

November 20

a writer's path

The writer's path is made of
stepping stones of
    concentration
    commitment
    awareness
    loneliness
    faith
    openness to Mystery
    the breakdown of ordinary perceptions
It is about process,
    not destination...
about unfolding,
    not achievement...
And only in arriving
at the end, after telling one's
own story, can one turn around and
see the design & direction of
her life, and recognize it
    as "a path".

The least I can do is keep my eyes open. Attention is what I want to spend.
All of it. -Barbara Hurd

November 21

authentic

Authenticity-
    this is what I hear the voice
    of the Divine One calling me to...
        living authentically
        fleshing out, incarnating
            what I say I believe...
        being willing to be
            shaped into that shape which
            is most truly & fully mine.

Spirit of Truth,
   help me to BE me...to discover
   more each day what that is,
   who I am meant to be.
Help me to rejoice in
   the growing, learning
   process...to joyfully
   participate in it daily,
   in spite of discouragement
      (I am, after all, sixty-six)
            or pain...
For each day of my life
IS a day of my life...
   no turning back...
   only today to live & celebrate & cherish.
            Ever new life.
            Ever resurrection.
            Ever & ever.
                  Amen

November 22

Some days mark us, remain with us forever. And we remember with clarity where we were, what we were doing...our minds and bodies retaining the memory of something which will never leave us, which will mark and reshape us forever...like 9/11 or the day John F. Kennedy was shot.

summing up

If I had to sum up
my life at this moment,
I would say,
      "Life has been hard."
And I would weep
with the pain-
      of a young husband's death
      of the death of my youngest sister
      of a bout with breast cancer
      of a disastrous second marriage
      of the death of my eldest son-
and begin to look harder
for the joy.

303.

November 23

This poem was first written in November 1995, two years after my eldest son's death on February 25, 1993, and then revised in November 2007. What amazed me, continues to amaze me, is how acutely the feelings return...the deep, physical pain which revisiting the memories recalls to the surface. The sense of loss never ends; the hole in the heart never totally heals.

to my son...

O come to me, my darling child.
I miss your voice.
I miss your smile.
My fingers long to touch
   your face,
to hold you close in
   my embrace,
      and keep you safe- protected, warm-
      a haven far from every harm.
But no- too late- my chance
is past- no more a boy; a
man at last who reached out
to embrace your life-
   a work you loved & soon a wife.
      How I rejoiced to see your joy!
And then, the phone call tore
the night. The words were uttered-
"Carl...dead...your boy
is gone...I'm sorry," and
the light went out.
      Down, down into dark and
      pain I traveled, there
      to dwell alone for months
      and years...
I though the pain was gone-
   but now the tears
   come yet again...
   and so I cry,
      O come to me, my darling child.
      I miss your voice.
      I miss your smile.

To grieve means to come to an understanding, finally, of inevitable balance; life will right itself, though how it does this remains, and will doubtless remain, mysterious.
-Alice Walker

November 24

which god?

How does God appear to me?
I'm not sure I have
ever known the
God of the Thunderstorm...
   an angry, vengeful God
   is just not part of
   my experience...
But the Mother-Hen God?
   Oh, yes! I have been
   gathered under those
   sheltering wings
      many times...
         held
         comforted
         nurtured
         protected
This is the God I know.

November 25

prayer for today

O In-and-Around-Me God,
   let me not jealously
   guard *any* position today...
Open me to possibility...
Let the words of my mouth
   echo, resonate wisdom...
Turn the kaleidoscope of
   my vision and help me to
      see new possibilities...
      dream new dreams...
      walk through new doors,
         across unfamiliar thresholds.
Help me to LET GO-
      and to know IT IS ENOUGH!

November 26

This writing was inspired by the Poem for South African Women by June Jordan, *which contains the beautifully inspirational phrase, 'We are the ones we have been waiting for.'*

sisterhood

Holy One, Mother of All that Lives,
   my heavy heart honors you today.
   As a woman, I live with the awareness
   that my voice is not honored in many
      places, even today, in this twenty-first
      century, in an age considered so enlightened...
   that the prevailing powers do not want
      to hear criticism or dissent from women,
      denigrating it as 'hysteria'...that emotion
      relegated to the female of the species and
      once 'treated' by hysterectomy...
         the removal of emotionality which so
         threatened the masculine, patriarchal
         world that it had to be excised...

Holy One, Mother of Creation & Creativity,
   this daughter of yours honors your life-giving
   presence, even as I struggle to birth it
      in my own life,
      in my own voice,
      in my own words,
   uplifting, supporting, affirming my many
   friends & daughters & granddaughters
   who struggle along with me to heal the
   hurts of this injured & bleeding world
   with our compassion & hope.
Together,
   we shoulder the load...
together,
   we share the responsibility...
together,
   we walk the difficult path
   of peace & reconciliation...
         for WE *ARE* THE ONES WE HAVE
            BEEN WAITING FOR!
306.

November 27

problem-solving

Sometimes the hardest thing
is sitting with the "I don't know"...
when every ounce of being
cries out, demands
           an answer.
            "Why?"
            "Why me?"
            "Why now?"
  The questions form unbidden
to what seems to make no sense...
    prevailing logic fails...
    and glib explanations
    fall away in face of
    pain & desperation,
    confusion & despair.

And though it seems inadequate
somehow, especially in our
need to explain & pacify & heal,
often the most authentic
answer is, "I don't know"...
    said neither as cop-out
      nor from cowardice,
    but from the depths of
      heart & soul...
        a sharing of brokenness...
        a meeting of weary
            travelers on the road.

*A horizon is something toward which we journey,
but it is also something that journeys along with us.*
-Hans Georg Gadamer

November 28

animosity
Sometimes I am my own
worst enemy, my own
jailer, my own nay-sayer.
How easy it is to blame
the 'less-then' aspects
of my life on someone,
something *outside*...
how easy to find a scapegoat
in circumstances of the past...
and to settle into the role of 'victim'
as I gaze at lives around me
with so much *more*- more money
                      more love
                      more intelligence
                      more fun
                      more talent
                      more...
                      more...
          more!
But now is the time for brutal
honesty. I fritter it away-
my money, my time, my opportunities
for fun, my talents. I bemoan
the stiffness in my joints-
        and do NOT exercise...
rue my book uncompleted-
        and do NOT write...
long for the joys of shared friendship-
        and do NOT pick up the phone...
Well, today I walked...and now I am
writing...and later I'll call a friend
about brunch. For this is the reality,
the truth of life: the power of choice,
of decision, of action, lies within me-
and if my life is 'less-than',
        I have made it so.

308.

November 29

One of my favorite holidays, Thanksgiving...a time for family to gather, a time to laugh & cry & remember...a time to celebrate the immeasurable gifts of another year of living. And a time to bake & eat pumpkin pie. Yum!

giving thanks

Today I offer

Heartfelt prayers of thanks,

Aware of all the blessings in my life:

Nourishing & nurturing family

Kind & supportive friends

Shelter- for my body, heart & soul

Gifts which ease my daily load-
      washer, dryer, telephone,
      a car to drive, a computer
      linking me to the wide world

Intuition, feelings, thought, the
   ability to reason & decide-
   gifts of intellect I all too often
   take for granted

Vision, hearing, taste & touch-
   amazing senses making me firmly
   aware of the wonders of this life

Nature & the glorious world of
   which I am a part

Ground of Being, Source of Life,
   in which I live & move &
   from which I draw my strength

     And so on this Thanksgiving Day,
     I offer thanks with my
     whole being...
         gratitude for all I have & am,
         today- and every day.
            Amen

November 30

*Heaven is right here on this precious spinning thought of God
we call Earth.* -**Gloria Karpinski**

AWE
amazement!
astonishment!
wonderment!
   so the dictionary, the
   book of words, says...
but that is simply
not enough...neither
captures not encompasses
the breath-holding feeling of
standing at the ocean's edge
at dawn and beholding,
as the sun rises, a family of
dolphins cavorting a short
way off-shore...
their sleek & lovely bodies
glistening, reflecting the
early-morning light as
parents herd their offspring
who leap joyously high with
youthful abandon...
For long moments I stand
absolutely still, transfixed,
enchanted by the spectacle
before me...
and only as they pass
from view and I turn to
walk up the beach do
I remember to
     breathe again.

reflections...

310.

DECEMBER ~
endings & beginnings

December 1

december

Outside my window,
the bare branches of the
Japanese maple,
its few remaining leaves,
curled and brown,
shivering in the wind,
announce the coming
            of winter.
But through the thatch
of branch and twig,
the pink-flowering bush
waves her lovely head.
I do not know her name-
    but every year she bears
    the promise of spring and
    new life, even as
            winter approaches.
Perhaps I shall call her
    Resurrection Tree-
    or Tree of Hope.
    The name- real or imagined-
    matters little...
            but rather the truth of her
            yearly presence and
            the beauty she offers
            in the midst of life's
            barren garden.

December 2

advent prayer

Early-morning silence
settles around me...
high above, stars shimmer
in the almost-winter sky.
Cocooned in this soundless
world, I let myself be

held, nourished, comforted
by the All-Sustaining Spirit.
Hope raises her lovely head,
scarred & slightly wrinkled
with age, to be sure, but
beautiful still...her smile
fills my heart with the
assurance of possibility,
even in the midst of
the world's pessimism...

The blue prayer scarf around
my neck reflects the color
of hope...the color of Advent...
the flickering candle at
my side sings of light
in the darkness as surely
as the far-away stars.

This, then,
is the fullness of time:
When the Son of God
is begotten in us.
-Meister Eckhart

As I begin this season of
waiting, of anticipation,
of hope, let my heart
be open...my eyes, my
ears...to see & hear &
feel the oh-so-silent
coming of the Christ Child
into our cacaphonous world.

Make of my life a cradle
to welcome & enfold
him...with every word
        with every act
        in everyone I meet.

Stir up in me yet again
the awareness that ALL
of life is holy...that hope
does indeed spring eternal...
that Immanuel is indeed
among us...and in us.
                Amen & amen

December 3

*What is the human? The human is a space, an opening,
where the universe celebrates its existence.*
-Brain Swimme

life's journeys

The flow of life moves in & through
us, taking us from journey to
journey.

And as I have been borne
throughout the years, I find
the flow of focus changing.

Where shall that focus
be for this third journey
of my life, the journey into aging?
On integration & transformation &
resurrection?
On letting the self come
fully into being?
On discovering at last the full &
complete ME in
all my glory?

Be undiminished, life calls to me.
Fulfillment awaits!
Live with full awareness!
This is the task of 'the final journey'...
at least in this here & now!

reflections...

314.

December 4

morning reflections II

Morning has always been
a special time for me.
Perhaps the stillness...
perhaps the sense of 'life' not yet
beginning, intruding...
the world at peace...
my spirit at peace...
 no noise
 no voices
 no complications
 a sense of safety & comfort
  of simplicity
Morning is rebirth
  another chance
  a clean slate
and I feel wholly whole in the
morning...integrated...not
pulled in different directions...
 ENTIRELY ME.

There is a gentleness to
my spirit...
  a thankfulness...
the energy born of sleep's 'death'
and waking's 'resurrection'...

Here I am, Spirit of Truth.
Use me this day.
Fill my day with creative energy...
let it flow into my cooking & from
 my words & actions...
let it surround & enfold me &
 all I love.
Cocoon me in your tenderness
so that I may be re-born a
refreshed creature with
 colorful & resilient wings.
  Let it be so today.

December 5

making sense
Perhaps it doesn't have to
make sense, this journey called LIFE...
perhaps fulfillment happens
precisely because it does not...
       because of its unpredictability...
          its out-of-our-control-ness.
It keeps us humble, keeps us thankful,
   keeps us awe-struck, mouths agape at the
      incredible, mysterious wonder of it all.
Perhaps the truth, the purpose
of all the meandering is to manifest
the infinite variety of emotion,
   of experience, of learning & information
to invite us to jump onto the human seesaw
and hang on for dear life through
      all the ups & downs...
AWE...WONDER...GRATITUDE...
PEACE...HOPE...
    all fill my heart
    on this December day.

December 6
*An honest spiritual life must have room for all our feelings
and be wise enough to help us look them in the face.*
-Alan Jones

grief's desert
My dear friend has died-
creativity has fled...
and my sense of abandonment
is very strong.
     God, where are you?
     Who are you?
     How are you?
I need you to be personal
         real
         present-

and all I feel is absence.
And yet, here I sit, talking to you,
    whoever you are...asking for
                your help,
                your guidance,
                your direction,
                your strength.
Lord, have mercy. All other words desert me...
emptiness swirls around & through me.
Are you in this desert
    with me?
or am I abandoned in my
    bereftness & sorrow?

December 7

What is important is to keep learning, to enjoy challenge, and to tolerate ambiguity. In the end there are no certain answers.
-Marina Horner

dangerous...

UNQUESTIONED ANSWERS ARE DANGEROUS.
I heard this somewhere...
    read it, most likely, but the where
    & by whom elude me.
It stares me in the face, this statement,
    confronting me...daring me
    to plumb its depths
    in search of truth.
And from those depths
    of mind & heart a
    fullsome 'Yes!' resounds...
    a ringing affirmation that
    any road paved with easy
    answers, any way which
    claims it has 'the Answer',
    is not the path on which
    my feet have ever led me.
For within me lives a
    questioning heart...
    a wondering spirit...
    a searching mind...

The way I tread is often
   two steps forward,
   one step back, with
   questing detours,
   yearning pilgrimages
   marking my wayward
   path.
The trek is seldom easy...
   with cliffs to be scaled,
   high peaks to be conquered,
   lonely valleys to be endured,
   but still I make my way,
   determined to live in
   the questions to my
   life's end.

December 8

Though my family is thoroughly German on both sides of the family tree, I am convinced that somewhere far back in time, we were Celts. For I have come to realize, in recent years, after a trip to the Scottish island of Iona, that my heart deeply resonates with the Celtic worldview; with the theology and cosmology of the early Celtic Christians. And I am finding this perspective spilling over into my writing, into my thinking & dreaming, into my experience of the world around me.

thin places

"Thin places", according to the Celts,
are where the world of here & now
rubs close to the eternal...where
visible & invisible worlds come into
near proximity...thresholds to
   divinity in our human world.
Christmas celebrates
the thin place that is
         the Christ...
   the flesh of Jesus of Nazareth
   as the conduit for the Spirit
   of the Divine to become manifest
   fully & completely-
inviting each & all of us to become
   thin places for one another...

God fleshed out again & again &
      yet again in us...
divinity shining through
humanity, manifest in
      who & how we are to one another...
                to our planet...
                to the least of these,
    as we kneel at the manger...
    as we live in our world.

The space between stars,
Where noise goes to die,
And the space between atoms,
Where the charges thin out:
These are places, too.
          -Stephen Philbrick

December 9

the Celtic heart

I have a Celtic heart, a heart
which knows 'redemption'as
the freeing of our original goodness,
    the blessing of our being-ness...
For, according to the Celtic heart,
we have been *spoken* into being.
We are creations of the Word,
    the poetry of the Creating One.
And deep within, so say the
Celtic poets, we are connected,
one and all, to Original Goodness...
    to the root of creativity & love.
At the heart of life is the Dark Eternal
Womb, from which all life bursts forth,
is born. And when we look into the face
of a newborn babe, we look into the
very face of God, for God is the
Life within all life...and holding this &
every infant, we cradle holy goodness
in our arms.

December 10

*A new calling can open the door
into the house of vision and belonging.*
-John O'Donohue*

a new calling...

How I wish that my cell phone
would ring and the printout
on its face would say, 'God calling'...
and the very voice of the Divine
would say, 'I have a task for
you to do, something which
only you can undertake.'

How I wish it could be just
that clear, and I could be certain
of my life's direction!

Before me lie so many paths,
each leading in a way worthwhile
and worthy of my time and effort...
each one with the hope, the goal
of leaving this world better than
    I found it...

Yet I walk in a heavy fog...
uncertainty obscures my view...
    which path to choose?
    which way to go?
    which one calls to my heart?
        and which one leads to home?

reflections...

December 11

It takes only a couple of seconds for a life to change irreversibly.
Suddenly you stand on completely strange ground and
a new course of life has to be embraced.
-John O'Donohue

a threshold

Do I dare to take a step?
To enter the mysterious
    unknown?
To leave behind the comfortable
    familiar?
Can I risk the passionate engagement
    of my heart?
the overwhelming complexity
    of rising emotions?
        fear, confusion, excitement,
        sadness, hope...
Am I willing to take my time,
   to listen with complete
   attention for the inner voice
   calling me forward, saying,
        'Now is the time'.
Do I dare to take a step?
To cross the threshold onto ground
    both strange & new?
To chart a course without a map,
    to destiny unknown?
Am I willing to embark on a
    voyage of discovery?
To live in such total vulnerability?
And, if life is to go on,
        do I really have a choice

reflections...

December 12

One of the most beautiful forms of Celtic poetry is the blessing: calling to mind and to expression those things we wish for and upon those whom we, at present, hold in our hearts. It is said, too, that the ancient Celts had a blessing for every activity of life, from the earliest moment of rising to the stoking of the hearth at nightfall, surrounding, filling each moment with an awareness and acknowledgement of the Divine infusing all of life. For the Celts, there was no part of life which was apart from God.

affirmation & blessing

I begin this day as
    a woman of faith...
    a beloved created child of the Divine...
    a vessel for holy love & light...
    a conduit for compassion & forgiveness.
I let go of all that
    has kept me bound.
I embrace the new day
    with gratitude.

May my every task be blessed with
    courage.
May my every encounter be blessed
    with peace.
May my every word be surrounded by &
    filled with love.
May I follow the path in front of me
    and so find *my* way.
                Let it be so.

your own blessing...

December 13

who am I?

Today I don't know
who I am. Who is
this woman living
inside my skin, I ask...
    who struggles to emerge?
    who longs to be seen & known &
        cherished for who she is?
    who aches to run & sing & dance &
        eat chocolate indiscriminately?
    who is so tired of being so
        damned responsible!

I want to be the joyful,
carefree youngest child
for a change...
    to shed my skin & emerge new...
            beautiful...
            larger than life...
            filled with hope...
            laughing heartily...
            twirling on tiptoe...
Who is that woman I see?
I look closer-
   "she" is ME!!!

in the mirror

My face is a roadmap
      of experience gained
      of lessons learnes
      of sorrows faced
      of betrayals borne
      of fires walked through
      of joys fully lived
NO APOLOGIES!
   'I yam who I yam..."
        Popeye & me!

December 14

december morning

Overcast morning- but
no sense of gloom casts
over my heart
Only the sense of peace,
of quiet without & within
Gentle sounds surround
and fill me-   birdsong
a breeze through the trees
the lilt of music
the quiet exhale of my own breath
the whisper of heat through the vent

Gracious One Who Creates,
grant me the gift
   of continuing peace this day
   of hope to uplift my spirit
   of gratitude for the
       holiness of life
   of laughter to lighten any
      load I carry
   of compassion for each one
      to cross my path
   of joy & a sense of completion
         when this day ends.

December 15

*Faith consists in believing when it is beyond
the power of reason to believe.*
-Voltaire

another resurrection

'Whom do you seek?' the angel at the
tomb asked the women. 'He is
not here!' And as I revisit the
deaths in my life, I find-
often to my surprise & awe-
that new life *has* happened...

often in spite of me...
without my consent or assent...
and in spite of dying again & again &
again, I keep being rebirthed...
my shape & visage altered
a bit each time, but the
person I am and continue
to become emerging...
walking into the future...
with head held high
even as tears stream
down my face.

December 16

A syzygy occurs when all the planets in our solar system are in alignment.
An amazing word...a fascinating concept. Can you get your mind around it?

syzygy

Align the disparate elements
of my life, O God-
the doubts & the certainties
the despair & delight
the faults & foibles
the unexpressed anger & misspent regret
the gifts I fail to recognize & honor
the procrastination & perfectionism
the joys & judgments
the mundane & mysterious
the profane & the holy
the brokenness & the wholeness
the laughter & the tears

Gather them all, Healing Spirit,
bringing body, mind & spirit
into alignment, that I may be
both blessed & blessing...
that my life may be a syzygy,
O God.

December 17

Within conception a deeper mystery is taking place in which life is issuing from the invisible realm of God into the visible world of creation.
-J. Philip Newell

birthing

Come, Holy Spirit...
Come, Spirit of Creation...
　　help me to birth my part
　　of creation into being.
Holy Midwife, fill me with the
　　inspired breath of creativity,
　　that I may give life to what
　　　　dwells within me.
Be with me as I birth the
　　thoughts of my heart & mind.
Hold my hand as I do the hard
　　labor of bringing thought &
　　　　dream to life.
Wipe my brow as the sweat
　　of my exertion threatens
　　　　to discourage me.
And rejoice with me at every completion...
　　every emerging bit of creative energy, as, with the birth,
　　　　I become a co-creator with you in the
　　　　　　on-going work of creation.

December 18

LET THERE BE LIGHT!

Come, Creative Spirit!
Come, Light of Lights!
Open my eyes...
break open my heart,
　　that my light may shine forth...
　　that my voice may sing truth.
Surround, fill & enlighten me
so that your creative energy
can flow through me.
　　　　　　Let it be so. Amen
326.

December 19

Tracks in the untidy edges offer hope,
the promise that the page might yield something
beyond its justified margins.
-Barbara Hurd

marginalia
I like to write in the margins...
to leave my 'mark' in the
books I read. And the more
marks there are, the more
the book has meant to me,
as I dialog with the author,
as I ruminate over her words,
consider deeply his point of view...

'Marginalia', it is called...
living outside the margins, the
carefully proscribed borders of
the print on the page...the place
where so much of life is
actually lived...sometimes the
best, most succulent parts,
the parts which prod & poke &
challenge, which cause reflection,
bring delight.

'Marginalia', it is called...
or perhaps, simply,
'living'.

December 20

follower
"Discipline" has
gotten a bad rap in
recent years, I think...
linked, coalesced as it has
become with "punishment"...
But to be disciplined is
to follow one's chosen path...

for a disciple is
a "follower"...
one who learns & grows
     by following the example
     and wisdom of another...
Perhaps we get it
wrong because there
are so few we really
long to follow...
     or who deserve our
     loyalty & respect...
        I wonder...

December 21 - The Winter Solstice

resistance

I read it somewhere-
I can't remember where-
     "Whatever you resist persists."
I must confess that when
I analyze the words and delve
into the thought that they convey,
     I don't like it much...
Yet, when I think of and acknowledge
all the things I have *resisted* in my life,
I find that often digging in my heels
did nothing more than prolong the pain...
    the doubt...the experience of that
    moment's anguish...which otherwise might
    have only paused- then passed away,
       leaving mere traces of its passing
       like footprints in new-fallen snow...
Life happens...an active verb...on-going &
never, ever static...the goal, I think, to draw
from it the learnings that cause growth
and lead to Hope & Wisdom, Joy & Love-
       those four Graces who show the way
      & lead us from resistance
       into Light.

328.

December 22

words

O, the sublimity when
another's voice coincides
with one's own...
when her thoughts echo
yours...
when his carefully chosen
words sing the truth
of your own heart...
            glory & grandeur
            pain & pathos
        released somehow in the
        daring expression of
        another's pen,
        resonating so deeply
        that all you can do,
        with tears coursing
        down your cheeks, is
        say, "Yes! Yes! Yes!",
        affirming the incredible
        meeting of hearts & minds
        rendered by words on a
        page...
            beautiful
            mysterious
            life-giving...
            a gift beyond
            measure...
        and once again, the
        Word is made flesh.

December 23

Christmas nears...and even in the midst of decorating, baking, wrapping, and savoring the sights & smells & sounds of the season, my heart turns often to something else...

something more

When I allow my heart
to break open, I find it
filled with pain
    for all the children who are
        starving around our world...
    for all the children who are
        being used & abused sexually
        for some adult's pleasure...
    for all the children who are
        quite literally enslaved for
        long & dreadful hours so we
        might pay less for *our* clothing...
    for all the children orphaned by
        AIDS and tuberculosis, robbed of
        childhood and of hope...
    for all the parents who must
        watch their children dying
        because they lack the money
        to pay for medication...
    for all the parents who cross
        borders at great risk & in great
        fear in order to give their
        children a better life...

> Surely I can do more
> than weep & pray.
> Surely I can!

*The inescapable truth is that whatever any of us does
affects all of us, one way or another.*
-Ted Loder

December 24

My youngest sister, Rennie, was killed in a car accident on Christmas Eve 1978. Though years have passed, the gut-level memories still exist deep inside, tainting my holiday joy with melancholy. As I was decorating the house yesterday, listening to Christmas music on the CD player, I was overcome by many memories. Not wanting to upset my mom with my tears, I held them inside...probably not a smart thing, but there it is. And this morning, this writing came.

this is life

Why am I so bereft? And why do I work
so hard to hide it? From whom? From *myself?*
Yesterday I nearly wept-
   but didn't...
      thoughts of my dad, my sister,
      my husband, my son flooded
      my mind as I listened to Christmas
      music and decorated the house...
Who was I protecting? Mother or me?
Sometimes I fear that opening the dam
   holding my tears will unleash a river
   of weeping that will never cease,
   sweeping me along like a piece
   of detritus over the rocky, dangerous
   rapids which threaten to destroy.
And yet, here I am...relatively whole
after the many buffeting storms
of life. Here I am...in so many ways
misshapen & scarred, but also beautiful...
   a curiously off-kilter vessel holding
   a slightly askew personality, my
   astigmatic eyes viewing the world
   both with incredible clarity- and a
   misty wistfulness,
      wondering at times about
      the might-have-beens,
      yet rooted firmly in the
      here-and-now...roaming in
      yearning remembrance, while
      walking steadily the mysteriously
      convoluted path which is my life.

December 25

Once again it comes, the celebration of the Incarnation...the coming of Divinity into our human world...the Manifestation of holiness in human flesh.

infinity...divinity

Infinity hides in plain sight.
Every leaf, every blade of grass
Holds a trace of,
Is a cradle for, the Divine.

Divinity enters life daily,
Incarnate in each newborn
Child, in every written word,
In every celebrating note.

The Sublime Holy enters
At the edge of every day
And dwells within the
Shape of dailiness, hidden
But accessible, awaiting
Only a flicker of awareness
To fully spring to life,
To add depth & color & meaning
To the everyday drabness of
Routine, of living dulled by
Trouble's weight, by sorrow's
Care, by anxiety's dark & heavy
Presence.

*As swimmers dare
to lie face to the sky
and water bears them,
as hawks rest upon air
and air sustains them,
so would I learn to attain
freefall, and float
into Creator Spirit's deep embrace,
knowing no effort earns
that all-surrounding grace.*
-Denise Levertov

And as the celebration of
Incarnation comes once more,
As we prepare to kneel again at
Infinity's rough cradle,
May we hear amidst the
Clash of arms, the cries of pain,
The wails of agony for broken dreams,
The distant sound of angel voices,
Bearing the hope of 'God With Us'
        to a weary,
                waiting world.

332.

December 26

Caretaker that I am- mother, nurse, pastor- it continues to be a struggle for me to separate myself from the problems of those I love, to see & accept that each of us must seek our own solutions, and that to acknowledge this does not mean lack of love or concern, but rather acknowledges the unique, innate abilities we each have within us.

problem-solving

I see you struggling with
a problem- convoluted,
deep, potentially life-changing-
and because I love you,
   I want to help...
      to fix things...
      to ease your struggle...
   but I can't.

As much as I would like
to think I have all the
answers, I don't...
    especially not for you &
      what you face.

For one thing I know-
  the answers must arise
  from deep within yourself...
  only then can they
  guide & transform
      your life...

Perhaps one of life's best
rules should be-
  no fixing,
  no saving,
  no advising,
  no setting each other straight...
   you sing your melody &
   I'll sing mine and, perhaps,
   at times, we'll be in
   perfect harmony.

December 27

I have discovered, you do not need to know what you are looking for-
only that you are looking for something, and need urgently to find it.
It is the urgency that does the work, a readiness to receive
that finds the answers.
-Janine Pommy Vega

improvisation!

The windy world without
reflects the windy world
within...
   the in-breathing of the Spirit,
   stirring up my life as surely
   as the wind outside disturbs
   the leaves & sends them flying
   helter-skelter through the air.
No easy answers come to mind
for life's hard questions...
no maps to limn the way
along life's tortuous path...
      for though I encounter
      teachers & guides of
      many sorts...
      though I entreat the
      Powers-That-Be to
      set my feet where I
      should tread...
      though I long for
      a way of ease & stark
      simplicity spelled out
      for me in certain terms...
         when I stop the frantic searching...
         when I take time to listen...
         when I pause to let the Truth sink in...
           the Voice I hear from
           deep inside calls,
              "Improvise!!!"

December 28

prayer for today

O, In-and-Around-Me God,
   let me not jealously
   guard *any* position today...
Open me to possibility...
Let the words of my mouth
   echo, resonate wisdom...
Turn the kaleidoscope of
   my vision and help me to
   see new possibilities...
   dream new dreams...
   walk through new doors,
       across unfamiliar thresholds.
Help me to LET GO-
      and to know IT IS ENOUGH!

December 29

Real prayer plunges us into life, red and raw. It gives us new eyes.
It shapes a new heart within us. It leaves us breathless in the presence
of the living God. It makes demands on us- to feed the hungry and
clothe the naked, give drink to the thirsty and take care of the sick.
It requires that we become the hands of the God
we say we have found.
-Joan Chittister

prayer

If prayer is sending love & light &
   blessing out into the world-
      which I believe it is-
if prayer is willingly giving part of
   yourself to another, to the world-
   rather than entreaty or plea-
shouldn't that effect the way we
   "do" prayer in the church?
"Lord, hear our prayer," we ask-
   as if God *needs* our pleading,
   our requests, our prodding to
   be made aware of the realities
   of human need,

planetary problems,
nature's distress.
Is prayer about changing the
mind & heart of God-
or our own?
and if we lay it all in the lap
of God, aren't we letting
ourselves off the hook?

December 30

*...if I put this off and wait until I'm older,
what if I don't make it to being older?*
-Stephan Brown

celebration

Nearly gone,
these twelve months...
slipping away to
join all those gone
before. Another year
of living, now a part of
the past- yet also here
in my present, still
enlivening my future.
Nothing wasted, I am told...
nothing left behind...each
experience part of the
becoming that is my life...

Here I stand on the
brink of a new year,
simultaneously the same &
different from the woman
I was at the beginning
of this year...
dwelling in the miasma
of discouragement & joy,
sadness & hope, doubt &
faith, mystery & uncertainty...

So ring the bells!

Sound the horns!
Drop the ball in Times Square!
Offer a champagne toast
    to the New Year!
        And shed a tear for
        what has been lost,
        never to be recovered...
        five hundred twenty-five
        thousand six hundred
        minutes of my life...
                gone & gone & gone-
                    and how do I celebrate
                    that?

December 31 - midnight

new year prayer
A tentative, tiny baby
step into the New Year...
    What lies ahead,
    I wonder...
        around the next corner?
        beyond the distant hill?
    What promise?
    What hope?
    What decisions?
    What experiences?

Here I am, God of Life,
teetering on the edge
of another year- yet
fully aware that all this
talk of dates and time are
simply ways of labeling
what we cannot grasp-
        timelessness...
        eternity...

"A thousand ages in your
sight are like an evening gone..."
the hymnist wisely sang...

And tomorrow, though the calendar
will speak of major change-
another year begun anew-
I will simply put one foot in
front of the other to continue
the journey begun these many
years ago, holding ever more
tightly to your comforting
hand.

    As the New Year approaches,
    be my vision...my guide...my light...
    that the darkness may not overwhelm me...
    that the wonder of the sun's light may
                brighten my world
                anew. Amen & amen

reflections...

About the author:

The author, Linda Faltin, has been on her life journey for sixty-six years. Along the way, she has been mother of four, grandmother of five; nurse, hospice director, ordained Lutheran pastor. She has lived through many losses: the death of her thirty-seven-year-old husband, of her twenty-five-year-old sister, of her twenty-eight-year-old son. She is also a twenty-four year survivor of breast cancer. She is a native Pennsylvanian but for the past 23 years has been a resident of North Carolina. She is the author of *Captain Booby Trap: One Man's Memories* and *New Day Dawning: Everyday Encounters with the Holy.*

Printed in the United States
131486LV00003B/136-198/P